A.D.D.
WELCOME to our WORLD

A Positive Perspective on Attention Deficit Disorder

Cynthia Calvert-Phillips

with her husband

Phil Phillips

CASSCOM Media

A.D.D.
Welcome to Our World
by Cynthia Calvert-Phillips and Phil Phillips
Published and distributed in conjunction with Casscom Media

ISBN 193003498-9

Printed in the United States of America

Cover design: Joe Potter, www.graphiks.com

Interior design: Lynn Copeland, design@genesis-group.net

Unless otherwise noted, Scripture quotations are from THE NEW KING JAMES VERSION. © 1979, 1980, 1982 by Thomas Nelson, Inc. Publishers. Used by permission.

Scripture quotations noted The Message are from THE MESSAGE. © 1993, 1994, 1995, 2000, 2001, 2002 by Eugene H. Peterson. Used by permission of NavPress Publishing Group.

Scripture quotations noted NIV are from THE HOLY BIBLE, NEW INTERNATIONAL VERSION. © 1973,1978, 1984 by International Bible Society. Used by permission of Zondervan Bible Publishers.

Scripture quotations noted RSV are from THE REVISED STANDARD VERSION. © 1946, 1971 by the National Council of Churches. Used by permission.

Scripture quotations noted KJV are from the King James Version of the Bible.

Scripture quotations noted NLT are from the *Holy Bible*, New Living Translation, © 1996. Used by permission of Tyndale House Publishers, Inc., Wheaton, Illinois 60189. All rights reserved.

For information regarding special discounts for bulk purchases for sales promotions, premiums, fund-raising, or educational use, please contact:

Miracle Families
P.O. Box 2333
Rockwall, Texas 75087
Toll-free in the USA: 1-877-633-3005
Fax: 972-722-1721
miraclefamilies@mac.com
www.miraclefamilies.net

If you would like the audio version of this book, contact your local Christian bookstore, or purchase it at www.Casscommedia.com.

Contents

5

Introduction

The shrill of the alarm clock jolts me from a short night of rest. Panic sets in as I discover it was incorrectly set the night before by my husband. Necessity moves us to quickly leap in the shower together to save time, fearful of missing our early morning flight. In a rush to leave for the hour commute to the airport, Phil can't seem to remember where he laid the car keys the night before. No problem, we'll use my set and worry about his later.

Miraculously, two hours later, we enjoy a quick but satisfying breakfast at T.G.I. Friday's in the Dallas/Ft. Worth International Airport, only to discover that my husband has misplaced our tickets. Panic would look to return for the second time in one morning but, fortunately, the additional copy I have tucked away in our bag saves us.

As we climb on the plane, we squeeze into our assigned seats. The nervous soul seated across from us watches as we cram our overstuffed bags into the luggage compartment. Phil prepares for the three-hour flight to Oakland, removing his Macintosh computer, his freshly updated iPod, and numerous *Mac Addict* magazines. We are on our way.

An hour into the flight, beverages are served and, as Phil attempts to pass my drink, he knocks his elbow against the seat, spilling the drink on himself and mostly on my freshly dry-cleaned khakis. The steward reluctantly hands him another drink, and hallelujah, another drink in my lap. The thought went through my mind, *It could be worse, we could be flying to Japan.*

Hours later we land and Phil dutifully begins to remove our luggage from the overhead compartment. Unaware of the petite, elderly lady standing behind him, he unknowingly elbows her between the eyes, with what I think later became at least a small "bruiser" of which she can be proud. I offer her an apologetic nod on his behalf.

Leaving a trail of Diet Coke stains and injured old ladies, we join the herd of fellow passengers making their way to baggage claim. (However, I did notice a couple of passengers from our section lagging behind, probably in an effort to avoid being punched.) After checking to see if we had our mound of books, equipment, and overly packed wardrobe, we had indeed made it to Oakland.

The pastor of the church where we were speaking met us at the airport. Upon seeing Phil for the first time, the pastor was immediately intrigued by his 6'4", heavyweight-wrestler, off-season size. Phil's long hair and scruffy beard hardly made matters easier for the neatly groomed pastor, who sported a blue blazer and khaki pants (with no Diet Coke stains on them). I prepared myself for the norm—my daily, sometimes hourly feat of helping others understand this man, affectionately referred to as The Gentle Giant or Shrek.

As our unsuspecting host drives us to our hotel, my husband, in a sincere effort to make conversation, finds himself, as usual, interrupting with such fervor so as to not allow the host to complete a full sentence. From the back seat, I gently lay a hand on Phil's shoulder to try to unobtrusively bring to his attention his lack of sensitivity. He

8

lovingly lays his hand on mine, enjoying the sweet act of affection on my part. Oh well, we have the entire weekend to discuss social graces.

Our host actually seemed intrigued listening to Phil's deep insights and knowledge on a variety of subjects. Even I, at times, find myself pleasantly surprised at how my husband knows so much about so many things. Then I remind myself that people with an IQ of 180 usually do know a lot.

Once in our hotel room, we remember to call and check in on our four teenagers. We jointly agree to use our cell phone since the long distance is included. I open the computer bag only to discover no cell phone—only the phone charger. Upon my inquisition of where the cell phone might be, and after a laborious retracing of our steps that day, my husband remembers taking it out on the plane to turn it off, and placing it in the seat pocket in front of him. A surreal vision came to me of our cell phone heading to Japan.

We managed to check on the kids, deciding then to turn in for the night. Just as I start to doze off, I begin feeling as though I'm in one of those cheap (really cheap) hotels that offer vibrating beds for a quarter. (I've actually never been in one of those kinds of hotels and often wonder if they really exist.) Nonetheless, a familiar rhythmic motion is driving me to near motion sickness—it is the dreaded "shaky leg syndrome." In his usual way of trying to unwind, relax, and in some cases fight boredom, my husband rhythmically moves his leg to the beat of a newborn rabbit's heart rate, and that rabbit was a-hoppin'.

Realizing the leg shaking would fail to rock him to sleep, he decides to get up and take a long, hot relaxing bath. Trying not to wake me, Shrek slowly creeps to the bathroom, reaches for a towel, and

9

knocks the mouthwash onto the floor. I could tell by his subsequent movements that earlier he had forgotten to put the lid on the mouthwash, and was now searching for a towel to clean up the mess. So much for my nice shower in the morning. Of course, drying off to the scent of wintergreen might not be so bad.

At last, I hear successful sounds of bath water running. My husband will soon return to bed, curl up next to me, and fall into a much needed and deserved sleep. I turn over, smiling to myself, silently applauding another day in the world of ADD.

10   It has been almost twelve years since we found out that my husband, Phil, had Attention Deficit Disorder (ADD). I am constantly amazed at how many people relate to our very real stories such as this one. Not every day holds such drama, but there are enough of those days to motivate me to write this book. It has been a long journey to get to the place where we can laugh at ourselves and enjoy each other's God-given differences. And as you will see in *Welcome to Our World*, the journey was not always easy.

My husband and I now conduct seminars for churches and organizations, teaching people about ADD. It's not unusual at these seminars for at least one unsuspecting soul to get an elbow in the ribs or a pair of eyes rolled their direction by their seatmate. Finding out you are ADD as an adult hits home with a lot of people. After sitting through our two-hour seminar, some attendees leave with more questions than answers. Some laugh at themselves, while others are in tears, realizing for the first time that they are understood and are not alone.

Welcome to Our World is a reflection of how deeply ADD has affected my husband, our family, and our lives. Although the book is penned by me, rest assured that Phil has offered himself as the main illustration throughout, requiring much courage and transparency. It is a book of hope—the only one of its kind that takes into consideration God's perspective on what has become a confusing subject in our society. It is written with the intent that no one needing real answers to real concerns should have to laboriously sift through contradictory theories on ADD, read numerous books, or spend endless hours on the Internet searching for help with ADD.

Through this book you will find answers to hard questions that clarify many issues surrounding ADD. And more importantly, you will discover you are not alone—whether you are the one who has ADD or are the spouse, family member, or friend of an ADD individual. Regardless of your status, we offer you a glimpse into the very real world of ADD.

Welcome.

CHAPTER ONE
Framing ADD

"Whatever you are, be a good one."
—ABRAHAM LINCOLN

CYNTHIA CALVERT-PHILLIPS

Some years ago a young man came to us for pastoral counseling. At the time, he was the youngest assistant fire chief in the nation. Sharp, good-looking, and well educated, he had a great heart and love for his family and God. He and his wife had been separated for nine months when they asked if we would meet with them.

After three hours of trying to figure out why this couple could not even agree on what day of the week it was, we were prompted to ask the husband a couple of pointed questions. The questions were simple, yet very telling: "Do you often lose things such as your wallet, checkbook, or keys?" He not only answered in the affirmative, but his wife chimed in saying, "Always, every day!"

We continued our questioning: "Are you easily distracted?" Again, the wife quickly answered for him, accusing the chief of often getting lost on the way home from work!

The next minute would become one of the most poignant moments in our ministry as this young, energetic fire chief rolled up his shirt sleeve, and with tears in his eyes replied, "Look at my watch. It is also a compass. Yes, I sometimes get distracted and miss my exit coming home. I'm the brunt of jokes at work because I am not even allowed to drive my own fire truck for fear of losing my sense of direction."

Attention Deficit Disorder, or ADD, is certainly a hot topic in our society. The pendulum of opinion, ideas, and beliefs on ADD swing from one spectrum to the other. Many believe it a myth; others consider it a brain disorder. To some, it is over-diagnosed; to others underdiagnosed. Medicating the condition is as controversial as the condition itself.

There is much confusion about the issue—what it is, what to do about it, what not to do, and so on. Consider the following definitions of ADD taken from various medical sources:

- A pervasive symptom complex involving inattention, impulsiveness, distractibility, and hyperactivity

- A neurobiological disorder with symptoms caused by a chemical imbalance in the brain

- A pathological condition, a genetic illness

- A phantom disorder

- A psychiatric disorder

- Einstein's Disease

- A brain disorder

It seems that even the medical community cannot agree on a conclusive definition, thus the term Attention Deficit Disorder remains the name given (albeit a substandard one, as we will discuss throughout the book). For those who exhibit excess energy or hyperactivity, along with the other symptoms of ADD, the applied term is ADHD (Attention Deficit Hyperactivity Disorder). For the purpose of this book, however, we will refer only to the term ADD rather than ADHD, since many individuals who have other characteristics of ADD are not hyperactive or the hyperactivity has decreased with age.

Most in the medical field would agree that the brain of an ADD person works and reacts differently from that of "normal" people. The commonly accepted belief is that in an ADD person the frontal lobe of the brain does not receive an adequate amount of stimulation. This would certainly explain the need to seek out stimulation, engage in risky behavior, or become easily distracted. There are some tests that doctors claim can actually show this difference in the brain of the ADD individual. The jury is still out among medical professionals regarding whether this claim is accurate.

15

The fact is, as of this writing, scientists have yet to fully explain what is occurring in the brain of a person who exhibits ADD characteristics. This only proves that the popularity of an idea does not give it scientific validity. There are many theories on ADD, and at times these theories overlap. For example, one supposition is that ADD has a genetic basis but is also a neurobiological disorder.

Some books about ADD quote philosopher Ivan Illich as having said, "Each civilization defines its own diseases. In other words, what is sickness in one might be abnormality, crime, holiness, or sin in another. For the same symptom of compulsive stealing in different communities one might be executed, tortured to death, exiled, hospitalized, or given alms or tax money."

Not only do cultures and societies define disorders and diseases differently, but generations do as well. What one generation considers abnormal, another generation may accept as quite normal. Years ago, homosexuality was considered to be a disease or a mental illness. Today, the American Psychiatric Association has decided that it is not. On the flip side of the coin, there are numerous characteristics of human behavior that were considered normal twenty, thirty, even a hundred years ago, but are today defined as a mental illness. In our opinion, ADD and ADHD may fall under the category of behavior defined by context. One should consider if the person who exhibits ADD characteristics could function perfectly in a different surrounding or culture as opposed to our North American mindset and lifestyle.

After years of extensive research and study, along with our personal experience in dealing with ADD, our conclusion regarding the phenomenon of ADD is one that may or may not line up with the medical field. Our view is that ADD is probably both a brain disposition and a variance of a God-given personality. It is often used as an excuse for bad behavior, likely overdiagnosed in children, underdiagnosed in adults, overmedicated in children, and probably undermedicated in adults.

Our sole purpose, however, is not to challenge theories on whether ADD is a genetic disease, a brain disorder, or a crutch for lazy and undisciplined people. Rather, it is to deliver help in a practical and biblical way to a large sector of people in our society who are severely misunderstood, negatively labeled, and in need of some solid, practical answers. Regardless of what our individual opinions or theories might be, there is a large enough populace (some believe as many as 20 to 30 percent of Americans) who exhibit the same characteristics of ADD to merit offering hope in a positive perspective.

Characteristics of ADD

Although symptoms vary somewhat among ADD individuals, some of the classic characteristics are impulsiveness, inattention, distractibility, restlessness, disorganization, an inability to complete projects, and an unawareness of consequences for poor behavior or bad decisions. For many, if not most ADD individuals, these and other characteristics can cause irreparable damage in personal relationships, school, careers, and self-image. If how one sees himself is based on academic success, organizational skills, performance at work, social etiquette, and the perceptions of others, then it becomes inevitable that the ADD person will struggle at some point with who he is and his God-given purpose. Too often, the ADD individual isn't even aware that there may be an explanation for the persistent fog in which he lives. In fact, one of our closest friends, upon discovering he was ADD, described his euphoria in those exact terms: the fog lifted. In a matter of minutes his view of life became much clearer.

More often than not, the positive characteristics of ADD are completely overlooked or even denied. For instance, the ADD individual actually possesses, not a deficit, but an abundance of attention and simply pays attention "differently." Certainly there is no attention deficit in the eight-year-old boy playing video games or the forty-year-old ADDer surfing the Internet. Where the attention deficit may show up is when the boy must clean his room and the adult must balance the checkbook. It would seem logical that the same part of the brain is involved in each task—the desired activity and the less desired one. If the brain is what figures out complicated computer games, then is it not also the same brain that balances the checkbook? It is not that an eight-year-old ADD boy cannot clean his room or that an ADD adult cannot do paperwork; it is just incredibly more difficult and requires a different approach.

Dr. Paul Elliott, a medical doctor based in the Dallas/Ft. Worth area who specializes in ADD, wrote the following:

> From an I.Q. of about 160 and above, virtually everyone has ADD. Now, if that is "brain damage" as was pre-

viously felt, we should all be so damaged! Certainly it is not brain damage, and the sooner we acknowledge this, the sooner we will be able to take a more appropriate approach to ADD.

I encourage patients and their parents or families to view brain function in several unorthodox ways, not because that is the true way brains work, but because they effectively illustrate what we observe about brain function.

One is the Channel Method. There are two possible channels of function in the brain: Channel A and Channel B. Everyone in the world is born with a Channel A in his or her brain. This is the average channel and the only one which the majority of people have, those with the average brain structure.

About one-third of the population also has a Channel B in the brain and we refer to these individuals as having ADD. The people with ADD use Channel B because it is the only channel they can get to work very well. They have the "wiring" for Channel A, but they cannot get it to work very well for themselves for very long.

Thought processing in the Channel A mode is very linear, or mono-dimensional, and driven by time, priorities, tasks, and a desire for completion. It is as though the person were on a rail going all the way to the end, finishing the task, turning around coming back down the rail, finishing the task, and so on, back and forth in an orderly fashion.

Thought processing in the Channel B mode is very three-dimensional. It is not only fore and aft, but up, down, side to side, and diagonally, broadly ranging from horizon to horizon, and the floor to the stratosphere.

Even the most conservative estimates of those who are ADD in the United States would fall around 12 percent. Do we as Christians honestly believe that a very large segment of our population is defective? That only those who follow a systematic way of working, thinking, and relating to others are normal?

I recently developed a friendship with a woman who, though legally blind from a wound she suffered years ago, still retains some amount of sight. While I can drive a car, my friend cannot. I can walk across a street with no assistance. She must have a walking cane. She enjoys water painting, working puzzles, and even reading as long as the print is large. At sixty-three years of age, she is fiercely independent, a brilliant thinker, and would cringe if you told her she had a disorder. Challenges, yes. Deficit, no.

It is proven that individuals who are diagnosed with ADD usually have a higher IQ, are often more creative, and excel when it comes to thinking outside the box.

Even as Christians, we each face our own challenges whether they are physical, emotional, spiritual, or interpersonal. We each have our differences in challenges as well as in abilities and giftings. More so than in any other sector of people, Christians should be the most understanding and tolerant of those differences. Yet so many times we whose faith is based solely on God's unconditional acceptance of us choose to fall in line with popular beliefs that somehow those who are different are defective. In no other group setting is this practice observed than in many of our own churches.

It is proven that individuals who are diagnosed with ADD usually have a higher IQ, are often more creative, and excel when it comes to thinking outside the box. They are highly enthusiastic, energetic, goal-driven, problem solvers. They are the inventors, entrepreneurs, artists, CEOs, the warriors who dare to take risks. They are the ones who make life interesting and colorful, who dare "normal" people to change their monochromatic view of life.

However, in our culture, we have been drawn into a false acceptance of the idea that mysterious disorders, dysfunctions, and diseases are at work in our brains and minds. If someone were to add up all the many ailments and disorders we now have in our society (and if you believe the statistics), then almost 80 percent of the American population is messed up in one way or another.

This line of thinking stems from an acceptance of psychology as literally the gospel. The concepts of psychology (and its partner psychiatry) have so infiltrated the school system, courts, legislatures, workplaces, and even our churches and homes that we Christians accept hook, line, and sinker what these often liberal, secular humanists have to say. Yet, how many Christians can trace back the history of psychology and define its original goals according to its founders? We have come to accept at face value what oftentimes we know little about.

At the very least, our Christian psychologists and psychiatrists should hold their discipline up to biblical standards and practice it accordingly, being willing to make a distinction between what may be a true ailment and what may be a lack of spiritual discipline. Which behaviors should be blamed on biology and which have everything to do with the influence of the family, our society, and our choices? And honestly, is our society any better off now that we have become accustomed to labeling almost all behavioral issues as mental illnesses or disorders?

Applying Labels

I was visiting with a young mom after one of our speaking engagements, and she shared that her six-year-old son had been diagnosed and labeled as having ODD (Oppositional Defiance Disorder). This is one of the more current labels placed primarily on preschool and elementary aged children. I asked her some related questions, one of which was, "Do you think your son has a disorder?" She replied, "Not at all. I think he knows how to get away with things and I have allowed him to do it. He can behave when I am consistent in setting the rules and enforcing the consequences for breaking the rules."

While conducting ministry in Alaska, we met a mom who shared a testimony with the church regarding her ten-year-old son. He had been diagnosed as having ADD along with several other disorders. Placed on a number of strong medications, her son tried twice to kill her, once by choking her with the seatbelt while riding in the car. The problems continued for another year or more. Needless to say, their family needed some answers.

We met this family a few months after the parents had gone through our *Miracle Parenting* course. Once they began implementing the principles and concepts contained in the course, they saw a truly miraculous change in their son's behavior. In fact, on the night we ministered, the son remained at home babysitting his younger siblings.

We should be very concerned when parents too easily accept a diagnosis or label rather than looking at their part in causing or perpetuating the behaviors that constitute the "disorder." Now we are finding that if a child cannot overcome his Oppositional Defiance Disorder, he will subsequently be diagnosed as having Conduct Defiance Disorder (CDD), the label reserved for older children and adults who cannot or will not control themselves. Is this really the direction in which we want to head regarding our future leaders...future parents...future lawmakers?

There must be a point where the parent takes responsibility for the lack in a child's life (we will discuss more of what this lack may entail in a later chapter) and begin to immediately rectify the problems. Again, we are no better off by the onslaught of labels and diagnoses that have been placed upon us as a society and, in particular, on our children. The label of being ADD or having ADD is no different. It denotes a deficit, a disorder, and a helplessness that promotes a poor self-image and diametrically opposes how we were created:

Oh yes, you shaped me first inside, then out;
you formed me in my mother's womb.
I thank you, High God—you're breathtaking!
Body and soul, I am marvelously made!
I worship in adoration—what a creation!
You know me inside and out,
you know every bone in my body;
You know exactly how I was made, bit by bit,
how I was sculpted from nothing into something.
Like an open book, you watched me grow from conception
*   to birth;*
all the stages of my life were spread out before you,
The days of my life all prepared before I'd even lived one day.
    —PSALM 139:13–16 (THE MESSAGE)

22

Based on over a decade of research and study, we are convinced that the person who exhibits the characteristics of ADD possesses a variance in personality type that God created and wanted in this world. We prefer to use the definition *Affectionately Designed Differently*, and believe it to be a more accurate description of the lives of so many who have had the negative label of a disorder placed upon them.

While living in Costa Rica, our belief in the variance theory was validated. During one of our visits with a pediatric neurologist who specialized in ADD, this renowned doctor emphatically stated that rarely does a true "disorder" of any type constitute more than 2 to 3 percent of a population. He went on to confirm that when 6 percent or more of a segment of a population exhibit the same characteristics, it is not a disorder but is, in fact, a variance. While our beliefs were confirmed, it did not change the fact that the characteristics of the ADD person, while often misunderstood and wrongly defined, are also very real.

Family members, friends, and colleagues without a doubt recognize the quirkiness of the ADD person, but may not be able to put a finger on the problem. They certainly recognize being interrupted, having promises broken, or seeing deadlines go unmet. They fail to understand why this person, who has so much potential, inevitably falls short of the mark.

Just as visually impaired people must acknowledge and accept their difference and the challenges they face, so must ADD individuals. In other words, left unattended, ADD can leave a wake of frustration, fear, and failure that can often lead to other serious problems such as divorce, depression, financial ruin, drug or other addictions, and, worst of all, a sense of hopelessness.

In the following pages we will not only put a face on ADD, but will instill hope regarding the way people who have this unique variance see themselves and the world around them. Our lay opinion reflects our experience, knowledge of the Word of God, and living with ADD every day. This book represents the framework from which Phil and I originate.

In fact, much of what defines ADD for each of us is the framework from which we come. People tend to look at ADD through their own eyeglasses of life. For example, if you are into nutrition, then you will have a tendency to believe that ADD can be "cured" or at least tamed by dietary measures. If you are a strong believer in psychology, you will lean toward coping skills, professional counseling, and possibly medicine in order to treat ADD. Pastors, or other spiritual leaders, may come from the angle of ADD as a spiritual problem and may feel that it is an excuse for undisciplined or even backslidden individuals. A medical doctor may strongly believe that ADD is strictly a medical issue to be treated with medication. Teachers may feel ADD is a learning disability or possibly the reflection of poor parenting. Different frameworks represent different definitions and diagnoses.

Not long ago, I had an experience that illustrates this point. I had begun having severe back pain over a period of about a month. I had an inkling it was from sitting at the computer in a lousy chair for too long, accompanied by stress. I was becoming incapacitated and desperately needed to get help. Because we had recently moved to Costa Rica, I had no idea which doctor I should see. But my experience became quite interesting.

The medical doctor I visited wanted to treat the issue with strong painkillers and possibly surgery. The chiropractor was convinced that adjusting, popping, and stretching me would do the trick. A massage therapist recommended working on my trigger points, while a personal trainer said the problem was all in the way I exercised or lifted things. Even now, you may have your own opinion of what I should or should not have done.

On the way home from one of these many appointments, the thought occurred to me that all these professionals seemed capable in their respected field. Each made a great case for the answer to my problem. However, I knew instinctively that I had to pick and choose the parts of their diagnosis that applied to me. In other words, I listened to my body, used the knowledge that was given to me, and did what I thought was best in getting well. Of course, we are not suggesting that you should ignore medical advice, only that we must all be actively involved in our own health matters.

The issue of ADD is not much different. Many opinions exist on the subject, much information is available, but all may not be applicable to your situation. Again, each of us approach life through our own set of eyeglasses. The lenses may be framed by our education, our culture, or our religious experience. The one thing I did not do with my back pain, however, was ignore it, continuing to sit in a chair at the computer for hours on end. I had to make some changes if I wanted to see positive results.

Again, the point of this book is not to argue the differing opinions, advice, or angles from which people stem regarding

24

ADD. It is a fact that people can and will substantiate whatever it is they *want* to believe about something if they look hard and long enough. Rather, we deliver our educated opinion while offering hope for the ADD person and those who surround him, reminding everyone involved that they may have forgotten what is good about one who is ADD.

A well-known maxim reminds us that *knowledge is power.* We would respectfully add that it is not only power, but knowledge that provides us with safety, according to the book of Hosea:

> *"My people are destroyed for lack of knowledge."*
> —HOSEA 4:6

Interestingly, this scripture is directed toward God's people: My people are destroyed. Even those who have a personal relationship with God need knowledge in order to keep them from harm as well as to keep them from *causing* harm.

25

Positive Traits of ADD

Let's consider additional characteristics of the person who might be ADD. More often than not, these people are considered highly intellectual, charming, creative, inventive, and insightful. They are often characterized as having tremendous potential due to their high energy, creative intellect, and propensity for thinking ahead of the game.

Each day is a new day for most ADD individuals who tend to be quite resilient. ADDers possess an incredible ability to persevere even when faced with crippling obstacles such as impulsive tendencies, disorganization, and lack of focus. Often they have endured years of put-downs, teasing, nagging, and accusations. Statements such as the following may have become their internal dialogue or the voice of reasoning:

* If you would only try harder…

* If you would calm down…

* If you would only apply yourself…

* If you would keep your word…

* If you would stop daydreaming…

* If you would only finish a project…

An entire sector of people in our society feel alone, frustrated, hurt, and misunderstood. They are easily distracted, interrupt people, despise routine, have excess energy, and experience difficulty completing projects, keeping jobs, staying in relationships, and relating to people who are "normal." They are negatively labeled, and often end up living a life full of disappointments, failure, and pain. Frequently seen as misfits, they need to know that someone cares enough to become knowledgeable on their behalf.

You may be thinking that some of this sounds like someone you know, or even yourself! In either case, take a moment now to answer the ADD questionnaire in Appendix A. These well-laid questions will help determine whether you or someone you know might be ADD. If the majority of the questions are answered in the affirmative, this book is absolutely invaluable to you. After you have completed the questionnaire, we will continue our exploration of this unique variance.

One may argue that all of us, as flawed human beings, experience the same dilemma regarding many of these questions. This is true, but only to an extent. Anyone can lose a wallet on occasion, become distracted, or procrastinate in doing something you don't want to do. Each of us has found ourselves interrupting someone or blurting out something we should not have said. We all know people who can be impulsive or who act irresponsibly at times. Certainly ADD people have not cornered the market on locking keys in the car, interrupting others, or walking into a room and forgetting the purpose for entering.

The defining difference, however, is that while one might do these things on an occasional basis, for the ADD person *it is a way of life*. It is a daily and sometimes hourly struggle to be what most would consider normal. The challenges associated with ADD are a 24/7 battle. And more times than not, ADD individuals do not learn from their mistakes or failures. Somehow, many find the fortitude to go on, to try again, and to remain hopeful. But some do not, leading them to depths of discouragement and even depression.

If information regarding both the positive and negative characteristics of ADD is ignored, or you choose to live in a state of denial about this very real variance, you had better believe that you will have on your hands, at some point, much disorder and a great deficit. Of course the same is true for my friend who is legally blind. How silly it would be for her to refuse knowledge, tools, or assistance. Your lack of knowledge regarding ADD may have already created disorder in your life, leading you to this book. Again, it does not have to be a deficit or a disorder, depending on your choice and the action you take.

Perhaps you are the ADD person and are the one in need of knowledge. With the power and safety of knowing and understanding the truth about the way God *affectionately designed* you and millions of others, you will be rescued from the destructive path that may have already been set in motion. If nothing else, you will discover that you are not alone.

But there is a choice to be made: to read this book with an open mind seeking to discover an explanation for yourself or the person in your life who desperately needs answers, or to continue living in the fog that inevitably surrounds ADD. Both are choices. If you choose to deny reality, that is as much of a

27

choice as it is in reading this book and confronting the ADD head on.

Sadly, there are many people who would prefer to be "right" than healthy, allowing prevailing egotistic defense mechanisms to cover their naiveté. It is for this reason that we challenge you to temporarily set aside all your previously held beliefs and ideas on what ADD is, and seriously consider the information that quite possibly your Master Designer has put before you.

The fear of change, even positive change, in any area of our life can be paralyzing for some. Most people tend to change only when the pain becomes too much to bear. We don't want to see anyone continue to live an unnecessary cycle of disappointment, destruction, and despair simply because of a lack of knowledge. It doesn't have to be that way. You can wipe the slate clean and start over.

28

We believe in the God of second, third, and fourth chances and this is a *big* chance for you. Whether you are the one who is ADD or you are reading this book on behalf of someone you love and care about, this is a new day, a day in which the fog can and will lift. It is an ordained and appointed time as, possibly for the first time ever, you will begin seeing clearly God's design and His need for innovative, energetic, and gentle-spirited people who are truly *Affectionately Designed Differently*.

CHAPTER TWO

Coming Out of the Fog

"The opposite of maximized potential is a jeopardized future."
—PHIL PHILLIPS

PHIL PHILLIPS

I remember first feeling stupid in the first grade. Often brought to tears because of my difficulty in spelling and writing, I realized something was different about me. Knowing other kids in my class could write much faster and neater than me, I began to develop the lifelong habit of comparing myself to those who were more adept at writing and spelling—or at school in general.

It was during this introductory year of public education that the word "dichotomy" would begin to define my life: *Phil is smart. He is dumb. Phil is energetic. Phil is lazy. Phil is capable. Phil is irresponsible. Phil is sensitive. Phil is rude. Phil is not living up to his full potential. Phil has so much potential.*

I was younger than everyone else in my first-grade class. I was a good reader and very good at math—especially when it involved counting money. I memorized in picture form everything I read, including concepts. The teacher seemed to know that I was smart, yet scratched her head in trying to figure out why I just couldn't get the work done. (This would become the rule rather than the exception for the next eleven years of school.) All the judgments began by my school teachers, parents, Sunday school teachers, and friends such as *Phil is lazy, a daydreamer, he doesn't apply himself, he can't stay focused*, and I could keep going with all the negative assumptions that were made.

I was placed in the mentally gifted class, then taken out. I remember being "removed" from the class as though it were yesterday—the teacher had to help me clean out all my papers crammed in the desk. I was completely embarrassed and convinced that the school was now the enemy. Not even a year before, the psychologist who tested me for the gifted program told my father he had never seen another kid who could analyze problems like I could.

30

I had been motivated to learn until I had been in the school system for about four years. By the fifth grade, I stopped trying. I only did the bare minimum to get by. That would become my operating mode through high school.

As an elementary student, I was overcome with a desire to just get home, go to my room, shut the door, and watch television—all in an effort to escape what I could not control. This would begin my desperate battle in overeating to kill pain. Food became my drug of choice beginning an addictive grasp that would haunt me for years.

I learned to fake my way through school, choosing easy classes that would require little or no writing. In high school, I remember asking the guidance counselor which of the English classes would require the least amount of writing. I was told English Literature. In truth, the class required much writing. However, the day before the final, the teacher divided the class into teams and began asking for oral answers about the material. I answered 85 percent of the questions. Our team won based solely on my performance. The oral drill and the fact that the final exam was multiple choice allowed me to pass the class.

I didn't have computers when I was in school, and even now spell check doesn't help me since I spell phonetically. And again, my frame of mind from grade school through high school was to do just enough to get out. Several teachers in high school actually told me that I would never amount to anything. More labels, more accusations. *He doesn't turn his homework in. Phil can't stay focused. He doesn't try hard enough.* They all began to sound like the adults in the Charlie Brown cartoon whose talking sounds more like undecipherable squawking: *Wha-wha-wha-wha-wha.* Even though I learned to tune out those who labeled me, believe me, I knew what they were saying.

Much of my youth was spent in church youth groups where I was the unofficial activities director. I had the ability to come up with something fun to do, and people either really liked me or not—no in-between. Because of my Christian upbringing and deep love and respect for my parents, I never delved into drugs or drinking. I only ate and locked myself in my room.

My parents and I knew that I had some minor disabilities such as dyslexia—a common sidekick to ADD, although we didn't know that then. As a toddler, my peripheral vision never fully developed, requiring me to spend hours in physical therapy, crawling around on all fours at ten-years-of-age to better develop my vision. This was the only specific "problem" that anyone could put a finger on.

During the first few years of my marriage, I began seeing more clearly what Cynthia, my parents, and others already recognized in my life. I had difficulty doing certain tasks that others did easily, such as paying bills and returning phone calls, and had problems with interrupting people, buying on impulse, losing things, etc. All these and more began to have a serious negative impact on my life by the time I turned thirty.

I could live with irritating things like losing my keys, failing to close kitchen cabinet doors (my highest number is 18), or zoning out after a big project. Even Cynthia seemed to be okay living with the small, daily affects of ADD. It was the big things like impulsive spending, not finishing major projects, or forgetting important details that got to us.

Upon learning about my ADD, Cynthia's initial response was sadness, then excitement. She felt as though she had opened up the glove box and discovered the owner's manual to me. I, however, wasn't so excited. My first response was anger and withdrawal.

The most difficult part in learning about my ADD was bringing to the surface all the failed or missed opportunities. With this new knowledge of "who I was," I couldn't help looking back at all the opportunities afforded me, only to have captured 60-70 percent of them, if that. One missed chance—two, four, eight, twenty, fifty, a thousand—they have a cumulative effect. They are devastating and, if I allowed myself to dwell on them, could be paralyzing.

Today, however, I am miraculously dealing with my ADD through knowledge and acceptance; an understanding wife, family, and friends; and, yes, at times, medication. I say miraculously because God stepped in and changed my perspective on a lot of things. Yet, the memories of the prior days are still there, potentially stirring up deep emotions of pain and regret. I have learned that in the world in which I live, hope for the future may not completely wipe away regrets for the past unless one has complete belief and trust in God. I am grateful for a relationship with a loving God who can and does bring healing from the most flawed history.

I have a great family, a high IQ, a desire for success, yet my future was jeopardized because of my lack of knowledge about ADD. I came close to losing my marriage, my family, and my purpose in life because I didn't *know*. The terribly dense fog in which I lived has now been lifted. I now see clearly who I am, how I was designed, and how it all fits into the greater meaning of my life.

Some years ago, a scientific experiment was conducted on student volunteers. They were asked to wear special eyeglasses that turned everything they saw upside down. During the first few days of the experiment, total chaos accompanied the students —running into desks, bumping into others, falling down.

Soon, an interesting occurrence took place. Only days into the experiment, the students began acclimating to the special glasses. Yes, their surrounding remained inverted but they began accepting that up was now down and vice versa.

The scientists decided to continue the project for a month. By the end of the experiment, the students had fully acclimated to their way of looking at things. No longer were they feeling their way around or bumping into classmates. They could perceive distances, climb stairs, and even read and write, almost with ease. The students quickly adapted to their perceptions, even though they were looking through a faulty pair of glasses.

Again, we each have our own eyeglasses through which we view ourselves and the world around us. Our lenses of life may have been influenced by our parents and their values and principles, or by other family members such as a loving grandmother. In addition, other environmental settings such as school and church may have contributed to how we view ourselves and those around us.

Rare is the ADD individual who has not possessed a faulty pair of glasses his entire adult life. For those with ADD, their perceptions of life become reality for them. These perceptions, though often defective, have been placed before them by mostly well-meaning parents, teachers, employers, and society as a whole. The faulty perceptions have come to define their lives to where they have now acclimated to them. They live in an upside down world—at least from their perspective, and they have adapted to the powerful labels and influential tags put upon them since childhood.

They were told they were lazy; they now believe they are lazy. They were labeled as irresponsible so they must be irresponsible. They were made to feel stupid. They are now convinced that they are stupid. Without a doubt, when a parent or other authority figure continually makes a "you are" statement, it will become a child's "I am."

You are rude. *I am rude.*
You are dumb. *I am dumb.*
You are a space cadet. *I am a space cadet.*
You are insensitive. *I am insensitive.*
You are fat. *I am fat.*
You are a loser. *I am a loser.*
You will never… *I will never…*

When reiterated by teachers and other authority figures, the prophetic "you are" statements become more firmly entrenched.

34

Eventually, false information that remains unchallenged will become "truth." The lies that are told about us become lies we tell ourselves. These falsehoods become our own perception of who we are, the lenses through which we view ourselves.

An Upside Down World

The ADD adult has typically spent years struggling to sort the lies from the truth—to see things right side up. Many experience burnout; some turn to drugs, alcohol, or other destructive behaviors to kill the pain of living in an upside down world. Others go from job to job, counselor to counselor, church to church, and relationship to relationship searching for what they really do not know they are missing. All they have is a vague concept of the world being right side up. The quest for normalcy has worn them out, beat them up, burned them out, and brought many to a place of hopelessness.

When ADD individuals are confronted with a name for and an explanation of their "differences," they will usually experience some strong emotions.

When ADD individuals are confronted with a name for and an explanation of their "differences," they will usually experience some strong emotions. After all, years of being misunderstood, mislabeled, and misinformed are coming into focus possibly for the first time. The newly discovered ADD individual may go through an array of not-so-fun emotions such as anger, regret, or even guilt. But we must each remember that emotions remind us that there is something still alive in us—even those emotions that may be viewed as negative.

Just as any loss in a person's life has the potential to create regret, sadness, pain, and grief, so might the discovery of finding out you are ADD. We have talked with a number of divorced

35

people where one or both spouses were ADD but unaware of it during their marriage. The response is the same time after time: "If only we had known, things would have turned out different."

Often newly discovered ADD adults become angry with parents, teachers, themselves, or even God as they look back at many missed opportunities, failed relationships, or lost jobs. Part of the inoculation against these negative emotions will be the power and safety we discussed that comes through *knowledge*.

The adult who takes little or no initiative to learn about and accept this unique God-given variance will continue to experience frustration and despair. If one doesn't have a strong grasp on how to deal with the ADD, these regrets about the past will create hopelessness for the future. Hopelessness occurs when ADD individuals come to believe that their past dictates their future. And why wouldn't it? Those with ADD know all too well how to start over only to fail again, and again, and again.

36

The ADD adult may experience guilt from dealing with addictions such as drugs, pornography, sex, alcohol, cigarettes, caffeine, or food. For Christians, it is usually the addictions like food and caffeine. In other words, if you get caught dosing ten cups of coffee at the office, people don't think anything about it. If you get caught sniffing cocaine, you're hung out to dry, labeled as a backslidden sinner. In fact, in our years of pastoral counseling, any time we met with someone who had a problem with drugs, we always looked for signs of ADD. There is a strong link between drug (and other) addictions and ADD that cannot be overlooked.

Oftentimes, relief is the most welcomed emotion people experience. They no longer feel alone and realize that there are others in their world who are like them. There is an explanation for the way they are. It is exciting to learn all in one day that you are not stupid, insane, sick, or a bum!

Consider the myriad emotions that can accompany Adult ADD:

	ADD Individual	Non-ADD Spouse or Other Close Individual
Pre-Discovery Emotions	Feeling alone Misunderstood Frustration with self Depression Sadness Tiredness or burn-out Guilt Hopelessness Withdrawn Out of control Helplessness Low self-worth	High levels of frustration Confusion Fear Disrespect toward the ADD adult Anger Exhaustion Depression Hopelessness
	ADD Individual	**Non-ADD Spouse or Other Close Individual**
Post-Discovery Emotions	Anger Regret Resentfulness toward parents, teachers, and/or God Grief Relief Acceptance Hope Excitement Renewed fervor	Relief Regret Forgiveness Acceptance Understanding Excitement Hope Renewed fervor

Ideally, the goal for both the ADD person and the non-ADD person should be one of excitement at the true prospect of a great future. It may take walking through forgiveness for past offenses and getting beyond the hurtful emotions, but the journey will be well worth it.

Faulty glasses are so much a part of who the ADD person is, but they are an outward device that can be removed. Preferably, the ADD person will be the one to initiate removing the faulty glasses. And with the help of a loving Father, it can be done. Yet, if you're reading this book on behalf of someone who is ADD, you can be very instrumental in helping remove the faulty apparatus placed on the person you love and care about. For some, the glasses will be removed quickly; for others it will be more of a process. There is little likelihood that the faulty glasses have ever been of benefit, enabling the ADD person to see the truth for what it is. Instead, they have only created a blurred vision of reality.

One of the most devastating results from living in such blurriness is the loss of meaning or purpose in life. The daily struggle just to keep up with the simple things of life make the ADD person lose sight of the bigger picture. When you are constantly trying to prove you are not defective time and time again, it becomes so wearisome that there is little energy left for focusing on why you were put on this earth in the first place.

This happened to a close friend of ours who, because of circumstances in his life and the faulty glasses he was wearing, began losing faith. He began questioning not only God's presence in his own life, but the very existence of God. This went on for several years causing him to become listless, angry, depressed, and withdrawn from his family and closest friends. When his wife filed for a divorce, it was as though his free fall ended. He had hit the ground hard, yet the impact seemed to help remove the faulty glasses he had been holding onto for so long.

Today, our friend understands more and more that God is not the enemy and that He is, in fact, a perfect Father who loves us with a perfect love. It reminds us of Jesus' words, "Whoever seeks to save his life will lose it" (Luke 17:33). When we take matters into our own hands, it only prolongs the process of becoming who God wants us to be.

38

Many Christians simply cannot fathom God as a perfect Father. Some have difficulty because of their own father's poor example of unconditional love and acceptance. Others see God as "the man upstairs" who, while good in nature, is not actively involved in every aspect of our life. Much false theology has been preached that is diametrically opposed to God being a good and perfect Father who loves and accepts His children unconditionally. "God is good all the time" is more than a mantra we repeat in our churches. If we, as Christians, cannot define God's goodness, then it proves a great gap in our understanding of who God really is.

> *Until you have given yourself to Him you will not have a real self.*
> —C. S. Lewis

The Father's Blessing   39

God wants to bless us—not just in the sense of a "hallelujah!" blessing every now and then, but in a daily process of blessing. There is an immense difference between an *event* of blessing such as a baby dedication, a wedding, or receiving an unexpected bonus at work, and the daily *process* of blessing. In Genesis 32:24–29, we find a most unusual occurrence that gives us insight into this process of blessing.

> *Then Jacob was left alone; and a Man wrestled with him until the breaking of day. Now when He saw that He did not prevail against him, He touched the socket of his hip; and the socket of Jacob's hip was out of joint as He wrestled with him. And He said, "Let Me go, for the day breaks." But he said, "I will not let You go unless You bless me!"*
>
> *So He said to him, "What is your name?" He said, "Jacob." And He said, "Your name shall no longer be called Jacob, but Israel; for you have struggled with God and with men, and have prevailed." Then Jacob asked, saying. "Tell*

me your name, I pray." And He said, "Why is it that you
ask about My name?" And He blessed him there.

No one really knows for sure why God decided to get into a wrestling match with Jacob that night. Perhaps it was to wear down Jacob's strong will or help him release some pent-up frustrations! What we do know is that up until this point in Jacob's life, he was a self-made, self-serving, and self-directed man. Something else we know for sure—God was setting Jacob up to receive a blessing from Him. Another interesting thought is that of God knocking Jacob's hip out of joint—perhaps giving him a *special challenge* to remind him of his dependence on God rather than on himself.

As a young man, Jacob experienced an event of blessing, not the ongoing *process* of blessing. Just as the thief is never satisfied with his goods as the honest, hardworking man is, Jacob, because of his deception in receiving his father's blessing, had never experienced the full benefit of the blessing.

The blessing, in Bible times, meant far more than receiving a monetary inheritance or possession. It also denoted the father's love, acceptance, and affirmation of the son. In essence, it proclaimed to the son, "You are pleasing to me. You are worthy of my trust, my lineage, my love, and the profit of my lifetime. I am proud of you. I release you to be all that God wants you to be."

There is an ancient Jewish maxim that says, "The blessing of the father builds the children's house." Whether a Hebrew son received a father's blessing had a tremendous impact on his future—for if he never received it, he was considered unworthy.

The principle of blessing is as true today as it was when God gave it to Abraham. Just as Jacob cried out for God's full blessing, many grown children—in particular those who have had an ongoing sense of deficiency drilled into them—can't "let go." They find themselves bitterly holding on to deep hurt and disappointments. They consciously or subconsciously have a sense that something is missing from their life.

It is interesting to note that before Jacob experienced this profound blessing from God, he was never content with what he had. He was always competing for more. Jacob had a sorry self-image no doubt caused from some of his own poor decisions, but also due to his rocky start in life. In other words, when your mother gives you a name that literally means schemer and swindler, it sets the stage for you to live up to that name. And Jacob did.

But by this time in Jacob's life, he was hungry for what was real and what would last. He was tired of manipulating and making things happen. And God's response to Jacob's cry for help began by changing his name to Israel, meaning "Contender with God"—a pretty big leap from a traitor or con artist. One of the obvious reasons God orchestrated this dramatic, supernatural encounter was to remove the faulty glasses Jacob had been wearing, and give him a new pair of lenses—a new way of seeing himself and a clearer focus of how God saw him. *Jacob saw himself as Jacob. God saw him as Israel.*

After this life-changing encounter, we see Jacob trying to repair his relationship with his brother, Esau, by offering him gifts. Esau's reply was that he didn't need gifts—he was already a wealthy man. It is then that Israel responds to Esau as a changed man, a blessed man, a man with a new name, a new label, and a new purpose:

> *"You may have much but I have all that I need."*
> —GENESIS 33:11 (PARAPHRASED)

For the first time in Jacob's life he was content.

Mature Christians get to a point in life where they have a conversation with God that goes something like this: *God, if You never do another thing for me ever again, You have done enough already. I am content in just knowing You, You knowing me, accepting me, and loving me.*

41

As believers, this process of blessing is, in fact, that God knows us, He unconditionally accepts us, and He unconditionally loves us. Any doctrine, thought, or counsel that goes against this biblical principle is severely erroneous. It is the theological test of God as the Perfect Father. The ADD adult who has spent years as a square peg trying to fit into a round hole may have never felt as though he received this blessing, leaving him screaming inside, "I will not let you go unless you bless me!" He really may not even know what he is missing or what he is unable to let go of, just that something in his life is lacking.

While even a good earthly father unconditionally accepts and loves his children, he does not always unconditionally approve of their actions, and is willing to bring correction into their lives, proving that they are his. As parents, we do not bring correction into the lives of children with whom we have no relationship, although at times we would certainly like to! God, as our heavenly Father, is no different. The psalmist David wrote that God's rod and His staff (instruments used in correcting) *comforted* him. Loving correction brought into our lives is proof that we are loved and that we belong.

Unless those with ADD first have a clear understanding that God loves and accepts them, they will *never* be able to grasp who they truly are and what they were created to do. Approval, accolades, and affirmation from others, even from those who are closest to them, will never be able to fill the void. Only through understanding the grace of God is a person able to totally reject negative labels, overcome past failures, and conquer future challenges. This is the key for each of us in reaching our full potential in life.

A Clear Perspective

It is time for a clear perspective of how God views the ADD person. David, who exhibited the most ADD characteristics of

42

anyone in the Old Testament, was tagged by God as "a man after His own heart." God painted a prophetic picture of David's future by the label placed upon him. David the risk-taker, the warrior, the musician, the writer, and the visionary. Although he faced great challenges in his life, he was *favored* by God. He was preferred by God. God used him. God designed him. God chose him for a greater purpose. And in return, David refused to focus on the size of his giants, but rather on the size of his God.

God's view is normal and right side up. He sees the whole picture clearly. He did not intend for anyone to live in an emotional fog of an upside down world. This in no way minimizes the giants and challenges the ADD individual faces each day. But the Father gets it. He understands. He has a very clear way of seeing things. In the book of Jeremiah, we find a verse that accurately describes God's view:

43

> *For I know the thoughts that I think toward you, says the Lord, thoughts of peace and not of evil, to give you a future and a hope. Then you will call upon Me and go and pray to Me, and I will listen to you. And you will seek Me and find Me, when you search for Me with all your heart.*
> —JEREMIAH 29:11

With a new way of seeing things, a normal, clear view is now within sight.

CHAPTER THREE
Making Love Work

*"The best non-pharmacological treatment for
ADD is exercise, sex, and humor."*
—Dr. Edward Hallowell,
CO-AUTHOR OF *Driven to Distraction*

CYNTHIA CALVERT-PHILLIPS

I met Phil in 1987 in the foyer of what I consider
a great place to meet: in church. I was immediately
intrigued with his conversational skills, the way
he carried himself, and even his European style of
dress—strange only because we were in the smallest
county in Texas.

Finding myself drawn to this person's sense of
adventure, zeal for life, and certainly his intellect, it may have very well been love at first
sight. At the time, Phil, at the tender age of 24,
had authored a national best-selling book, conducted hundreds of media interviews and speaking
engagements a year, and carried an impressive
résumé, to say the least.

We quickly became best friends and, after knowing
each other for only several weeks, we agreed that
love had indeed fallen in our laps. After a short
engagement, we decided to commit to each other until
death did us in (and little did I know how hard it
would try).

Our first year of marriage was nothing like what
many others experience—no major adjustments in

living together or difficulty in getting to know each other. From the day we married, we were best friends, traveling, working, and playing together. We immediately started doing our share in populating the earth, giving birth to four kids in six years.

Our joint career included writing books, accompanied by traveling the country and world in an effort to promote the books. Life seemed pretty good during those early years. There was certainly never a dull moment for me, traveling by trains, planes, and automobiles, caring for my young children, and keeping up with a talented, energetic, and creative husband.

After almost ten years of writing and travel, we were invited to join our church's pastoral staff as family ministers, a dream come true for both Phil and me. We were ecstatic to "come off the road," enabling us to see firsthand the fruit of our ministry. We joined the staff hoping and believing this was the "final call" in our career, and one that would create permanency and stability in our lives. Both Phil and I loved the church deeply and completely believed in the senior pastor's vision for a growing ministry.

It wasn't until we began working for *someone else* that I became fully aware something was not "normal" with Phil. I certainly knew of Phil's impulsiveness, his times of seeming totally spaced out, and the problems with self-control in certain areas of his life. But everything balanced itself out with Phil being, in so many ways, a great husband, a very involved father, and in general, just a good guy. Any problems we faced early in our relationship we simply dealt with and I wrote them off as part of the fast and furious, crazy lifestyle we lived.

46

While working under someone else's policies, however, with different personalities and complicated staff relations Phil and I, and our marriage, began coming apart at the seams—spiritually, emotionally, and physically. It was during this time that I woke up one morning, looked at Phil, and said, "You are not normal." His reply to me was equally alarming: "If you are what normal is, then I don't care to be normal."

As the frustration, anger, and hurt continued to fester, Phil and I attended a marriage retreat specifically designed for pastors and their wives. We actually attended because we were becoming certified to teach that particular marriage course. (By the way, there are a lot of frustrated, angry, hurt pastors and their wives out there, and we were among them.) At one point in the retreat, couples were divided into small groups in order to discuss some personal issues. It was in this small group where, for the first time in my marriage, I realized that I did not truly know my husband, my friend, my partner.

Seated in a circle, the group leader singled Phil out and, for some reason, asked him if anyone had ever truly understood him or been able to *enter his world*. I silently knew the answer. Of course, I understood him! We had been the best of friends until we went on staff at the church. I knew him. I entered his world every day—though at times with fear and trepidation. I was there for him. No one could deny that.

Yet when Phil answered with a clear, resolute, "*No*," I found myself dumbfounded, confused, shocked, and absolutely devastated.

Phil continued, *"How could anyone understand me when I don't even understand myself?"* Whoa, this was not possible! This guy was raised by incredible

47

parents, was brought up in church his entire life, had good friends, and when he married me, he got a friend, lover, and business partner all wrapped in one. What did he mean he wasn't understood? He was blessed with opportunities galore while surrounded by people who loved him.

Some weeks later we held a symposium for the home school families in our church. The sole topic for the two-hour event was Attention Deficit Disorder. We invited three speakers: a lady who runs a school in the Dallas/Ft. Worth area specifically for ADD children, a nutritionist who specialized in ADD, and a psychologist who diagnosed and treated ADD.

As Phil and I stood in back of the crowded room, one of the symposium speakers began listing both the positive and negative qualities of ADD in children. (This was in 1994 when there was very little mention of *Adult* ADD.) My ears immediately perked up as it dawned on me that the large majority of the characteristics being recited were not solely applicable to some eight-year-old boy swinging from the church rafters. Instead, this speaker was accurately describing the thirty-something-year-old man standing next to me.

That night we had a nice chuckle about the whole thing, but gave no more thought to hyperactive kids, Ritalin, or ADD. We felt we had done our jobs by offering good information to questioning parents and that was the end of it.

It was two weeks later, on a Sunday morning, when the dam broke at our house. With an already strained relationship, we got into a heated "discussion" on the way to church. I do not remember what the argument was about. I do know, however, that we were not happy in our relationship, with our family life, or with our jobs. And now we found ourselves having to put on the pastoral "happy

48

face" for two very long Sunday morning services. Somehow we survived church (or I should say somehow they survived us) and we came home to fall into our regularly scheduled Sunday coma.

As I found myself unable to fall asleep, I began praying and asking the Lord for help. I must admit that the silence of God seemed deafening during this time in our lives. Yet, as I lay whispering a plea to the Lord, the "thought" came to my mind to get up and go to the bookstore down the street. Although I read three to five books a week, I do not usually get them in regular bookstores. However, I was definitely drawn to this particular bookstore.

As I entered the store, I am sure the young guy behind the counter didn't know what hit him. Frantic, I reached across the counter, placed both my hands on his shoulders, and demanded that he give me anything he had on Adult ADD. Again, it was years before the general public ever heard the term *Adult* ADD. Most considered ADD a kid's problem and believed that kids outgrew ADD. Fortunately, the employee said that he had one book and nervously rushed to get it for me.

49

That afternoon, I sat in the bookstore reading one of the first books ever written on the subject of Adult ADD, and began weeping. I could not believe my eyes. In front of me was an owner's manual to my husband whom I thought I knew so well. It would forever change me, my life, and certainly the life of Phil Phillips.

As the full depiction of my husband's life began coming into clearer focus for me, the only word that could describe it was *dichotomy*. This word, for some strange and unknown reason, had defined every aspect of who Phil was, what he did, and how he lived:

Phil is the most sensitive guy in the world. He knows how to laugh, cry, encourage, correct, and minister to the needs of others—all at the same time.

This guy is rude, constantly interrupts people, can talk incessantly, and will say whatever is in his head at the moment, with seemingly no regard for the person whose ears the words fall upon.

He is responsible. Signing contracts with book publishers, getting the deal done, providing for his family, working hard, and taking time for the kids and me. He has always been there for us.

He cannot manage a checkbook. In fact, he can't find his checkbook most of the time. He buys twelve pairs of socks when he only needs two, has problems sticking with long-term projects, and gets so distracted while driving that he misses familiar exits.

50

He is, without a doubt, smart. Testing out at a genius IQ, Phil can hold a conversation about anything, with anyone. Creative, with an excellent grasp of the English language, Phil is someone who commands an audience, regardless.

I remember when Phil and I were engaged, and he sent me a card. Inside it read: "I love you with all my hart. We have a grate futur ahead of us." I sloughed off the misspelling in the note, thinking he was in a hurry as he wrote it. However, as the years progressed, I came to realize that Phil, although having mastered the use of the English language, spelled on about a sixth-grade level.

Phil is a hard worker. While he was on the road, he would put in long, hard days. One month he drove over seven thousand miles. There was no question that he was motivated in his ministry, gave 100 percent, and was good at what he did. He definitely tried hard and succeeded often.

At times, Phil became overwhelmed, exhausted, and mentally paralyzed. Whether coming home from a road trip, or ministering at a church on Sunday, he was what Arkansans would describe as "good for nothin'" on the following day. He can't focus, can't get any administrative work done, and prefers to sit at the computer or do some other activity defined as mindless. Most people can function, at least minimally, even after having a stress-filled week or working on a difficult project. He could not.

In looking back over our years together, I knew firsthand that Phil constantly lost things—his keys, wallet, checkbook. Once he lost $3,000 in checks and cash from product sales at one of his speaking engagements. Keeping track of bills to be paid, phone calls to return, appointments to be kept—forget it. Either I did it, or we ended up paying late fees and reconnect charges.

I was aware that Phil tended to do things impulsively. He made decisions quickly, which sometimes seemed to work out. Yet many times the decisions were irresponsible and detrimental to our family.

You are not normal. You are not normal. You are not normal. These words I had spoken to Phil came hurling back and, at that moment I realized, no, he wasn't "normal." With great heaviness in my heart that day, sitting on a wooden bench in the bookstore, I considered what an unbelievably desolate place my husband must be in.

Today, years later and much wiser, I no longer panic when my risk-taking husband challenges me to go skydiving, take a road trip to Costa Rica, or engage in some other harum-scarum activity. I'm learning to breathe, *really* breathe, relax, and enjoy in full color my life with Phil.

51

Living with ADD affects not only the ADD person. It is almost certain that the ADD person has lived for years in pain and confusion, yet those who are the most supportive such as family, friends, and coworkers are highly affected and share in bearing the brunt of the negative implications of ADD.

The challenge of overcoming the negative aspects of ADD is most difficult in the marriage relationship. It is believed that 85 percent of adults who have undiagnosed ADD will go through at least one divorce. Of course, statistics may reflect the truth of a matter while presenting a falsehood about what is *normal*. The truth of a situation does not always represent the way things ought to be especially according to God's standards.

On the other hand, the above statistic will not come as a surprise to many who are in a marriage relationship with an ADDer. The constant desire for change, stimulation, new endeavors, career changes; the empty promises, addictive tendencies, irresponsible behavior—any or all of these begin to wear thin after time and cause strain on any relationship.

Phil and I are living proof that an ADD marriage can survive and thrive. That doesn't mean it is always easy or doesn't require effort. Nor does it imply that Phil was the one who initiated what had to take place in order to bring our relationship into balance. It probably won't happen like that for you either. After we found out that Phil was ADD, we both worked hard at understanding each other, accepting each other's differences, and walking in forgiveness. But I was the one who first reigned in my frustration and anger, becoming an expert on ADD. I did it because I don't like negative statistics—especially when it comes to my family—and my marriage was close to becoming one of those statistics. I did it because my husband was physically, emotionally, and spiritually worn out from trying to be normal. I did it for my children. I did it for our friends and family. I did it for the person reading this book. Most importantly, I did it out my obedience to God.

Chances are the ADD person is not even the one reading this book, because the typical ADDer cannot finish a book such as this one. And that's okay; we actually wrote it with that in mind. If you are not the one who is ADD, then highlight the important parts and ask the person to read what you've marked (or better yet, give him the audio book). Throughout the years, I have found that it is actually more important that the non-ADD spouse or family member have a better understanding of ADD than the person who is ADD. And if you are making this much effort to learn about ADD for someone you care about, then you are one of the most important persons in the life of the ADDer.

In reality, however, many times the non-ADD spouse is exhausted and simply doesn't have the energy left to fight for the relationship once it has deteriorated to a certain point. It doesn't seem fair that after experiencing all that hardship and pain, this individual is the one being asked to, once again, make the effort or fix the problem. Divorce seemingly becomes much easier than sticking with the relationship and discovering the driving force behind the problems. Even after a viable explanation is given, the non-ADD spouse may be understandably unwilling to forgive the past and start over. More than likely that routine has probably defined the relationship. Forgive, forgive, and forgive—only to be disappointed by the next failure.

After so many "fresh starts," non-ADD spouses may begin to feel hopeless. They are tired of making excuses, cleaning up messes, and having to play the role of parent in the life of the ADD spouse. They frankly may not have the emotional or physical wherewithal to give it another go. Their mind, heart, and spirit have become hardened toward their spouse and possibly toward God.

53

I do not doubt that this is a picture painted for many non-ADD spouses. I have been there myself. You have been right on many occasions when your spouse made poor decisions. You have cleaned up messes time and time again. You have had to fix problems and probably resented doing so. Your feelings and frustrations are very real. You felt it was unfair. And you were *right*. The question is, do you want to be right or happy? Do you want to be right or fight becoming a statistic? It's your call and your call alone. Just as I had to make the decision to fight for my marriage (which included fighting for my husband), so do you.

Not only can the non-ADD spouse become overwhelmed, but when life remains blurry, it is easy for the ADD individual to throw his hands up and move on to something new. For many, that has been their mode of operation their entire lives: try something, fail, ask forgiveness, try again, fail, maybe ask forgiveness, try again, fail, give up. Eventually it can wear down even the most energetic, loving ADD person.

Regardless of which side of the fence you are on, you need to know that you are not alone. We have been there and so have many others, and we all lived to tell about it. Be assured, God will give you the energy and wherewithal to do the right thing for the right reason. We understand your situation and the frustration and hopelessness you may feel. Things can and will begin to change as you discover an explanation to so many un-answered questions and concerns.

Any marriage has its challenges, and it's common knowl-edge that 50 percent of marriages in the U.S. end in divorce. Half of marriages end within the first seven years and, sadly, 15 percent in the very first year. These statistics have remained true (though not *normal*) for years, even in our churches.

With this in mind I want to ask a question that will hope-fully set the precedent for the rest of this chapter. Have you ever wondered why 50 percent of marriages *do* succeed? How do half of the couples defy the odds? In a culture obsessed with sickness, disorders, and illness rather than focusing on wellness, it becomes second nature to focus on the 50 percent of marriages that don't make it rather than the 50 percent that do.

Furthermore, how does the other half make it when ADD is involved? What are the secrets necessary to hold together a relationship that may already have found itself full of hurt, disappointment, and frustration?

Obviously there are some key ingredients that all successful marriages have. These success skills, if you will, have been around for ages, perhaps coated in different terminology or presented differently than how we will introduce them here. Our "recipe" includes proven staples, along with some unique ingredients that pertain specifically to the ADD marriage. Problems in a marriage where ADD is at the root can look just like common problems in other marriages. The difference is the history of the person who is ADD.

55

No one would argue that ADD individuals are a different breed. They think differently, act differently, and view things differently. The "dichotomy" previously mentioned affects every area of their life and *has always* affected them:

- They are hardworking, yet seem lazy at times.

- They are responsible, yet forget the most important tasks required of adults.

- They are sensitive, yet can be rude, assuming, and moody.

- They can earn money, yet have great difficulty managing money.

- They are smart, yet do dumb things.

- Their sense of time is fast or slow, but rarely normal.

- One day they can; the next day they can't.

- They have difficulty remembering very simple things, yet have excellent memories for complex issues.

After so long, it becomes too easy to focus on the perceived laziness, insensitivity, and irresponsibility of ADDers rather than on what is good about them. And are they really irresponsible or could it be that they have genuinely tried, but for a lack of understanding in their own life, missed the mark? Are they truly lazy or do they work "differently" than others? Is this person a liar at heart or does he make classic ADD promises out of sincere intentions?

If you look deep enough, you will see the truth for what it is. It is easy to consider the negative qualities associated with ADD as character flaws when, most of the time, they are not. I know very few ADD individuals who are intentional liars, bums, or jerks. Most are simply misunderstood by those closest to them such as friends, family, and coworkers.

I am not minimizing the challenge of living with an ADD person. I live with one every day! My goal is once again to get you to recognize the good in the ADD person. Remember what drew you to your ADDer in the first place. When I look back at what originally attracted me to Phil, it was that his lifestyle was so completely different from my own. He had moved around and traveled the world. I had not. He possessed an eagerness to try new and different things. Until I met Phil, I always chose vanilla ice cream! He introduced me to a world of variety, change, and color. His impulsiveness equaled romanticism to me. Big dreams painted a picture of an exciting future. Phil's adventurousness was dangerous and very contagious—and I caught it! It is often true that opposites do attract, perhaps in a subconscious attempt to balance out our own weaknesses. All I know is that I was initially attracted to a wild man, and years later I would try to housebreak him.

And doesn't this happen in all relationships? After the newness wears off, we begin trying to change the other person. Too often this is caused by unrealistic expectations in our relationship—especially in our Christian marriages. We want to be happy, healthy, and whole 100 percent of the time. Yet what Phil and I have discovered in our almost twenty years of marriage is that about 10 percent of our marriage is made up of events of pure joy: a new baby, an unexpected financial blessing, a second or third honeymoon, etc. Another 10 percent is made up of pure hell: trips to the emergency room, financial drought, a fallout with a close friend or relative. The other 80 percent is somewhere in-between where we stay determined to make our relationship and our family what it is.

The same principle holds true in our spiritual lives—at least in the lives of the Christians we know. Around 10 percent of the time you can almost hear God speaking to you—tangible blessings come flooding in, goose bumps abound. The other 10 percent—you guessed it. Spiritual drought, locusts, diseases, and rumors of wars! Most of us live on a daily basis somewhere in the 80 percent zone.

57

We need to stop beating ourselves up for not always living in the top 10 percent whether in our relationship with our spouse, with our children, or with God. It is a way of demanding perfection from ourselves and those we are closest to. It is so much easier to focus on what we don't have or on past hurts and current problems than it is to look for solutions.

Rarely do we see a marriage, even an ADD marriage, that is in so deep a hole that the spouses can't dig out of if they are willing to look for solutions rather than dwelling on what is wrong in the relationship. If you want to get out of the hole, you need to stop digging and consider the proven solutions we are offering you in this book.

The Process of Blessing

In the previous chapter, we looked at the process of blessing and how it pertains to our relationship with God. This same process is also applicable to all the other relationships in our life, including our marriage relationship. It is vital that we take the same definition of the process of blessing and apply it to the marriage where one or both spouses might be ADD.

The Old Testament tells of David, the future king of Israel, who was the baby of his family, the youngest of seven sons. When Samuel came to town looking to appoint a new king, Jesse lined up his boys, somehow forgetting about David. (We know from experience that this is sometimes easy to do when you have a large family. Phil and I once valet parked our fourth child, so we understand getting caught up in the moment and forgetting the little one!) It is, however, interesting to note that even though David was overlooked at times, he was very secure in his relationship with God, giving a beautiful description of how well God knew him:

58

> *O Lord, You have* searched *me and* known *me. You know my sitting down and my rising up; You understand my thought afar off. You comprehend my path and my lying down, and are acquainted with all my ways. For there is not a word on my tongue, but behold, O Lord, You know it altogether. You have hedged me behind and before, and laid your hand upon me. Such knowledge is too wonderful for me; it is high, I cannot attain it.*
> —PSALM 139:1–6 (EMPHASIS ADDED)

The first element in the process of blessing, whether in your relationship with God or with your spouse or children, is having a deep acquaintance with the other person. Some parents can easily trace their genealogy back a hundred years but cannot name their teenagers' three best friends. It takes effort to get to know our children or our spouse, especially with the type of knowledge that David described and experienced.

In the above scripture, the Hebrew word for "searched" is *chaqar*, meaning to search out a subject or matter, investigate, or examine thoroughly. The Hebrew word for "known" is *yada*, from the root word "to know," and speaks of a deep personal awareness and understanding. It was God who knew us first. He knows every thought, every emotion, and every motive that we have. He understands every element of our being.

When we search and investigate in order to obtain this kind of knowledge of our spouse, it communicates that he or she is valued and important, and is not alone. This deep knowledge communicates blessing. This kind of knowledge takes us beyond each other's interests and abilities, and makes us aware of the other person's motives, fears, dreams, and convictions. This knowledge can, at times, be uncomfortable even in the best of relationships. This *yada* knowledge offers entry into the world of ADD.

The first element in the process of blessing, whether in your relationship with God or with your spouse or children, is having a deep acquaintance with the other person.

59

I thought I really knew Phil after almost ten years of marriage, which explains why I was so shocked when he said he felt no one had ever really truly understood him or been able to enter his world. I knew at that point we had some work to do in getting beyond the surface. I wanted to know him, *really* know him. I wanted to enter his world. I was determined to walk in the process of blessing my husband, which began by knowing him. I then had to make the decision to choose to *accept* what I knew about him, and what I would learn about him.

This is the second element in the process of blessing: the attitude of unconditional acceptance of your spouse. Again, there is a difference between unconditional acceptance and unconditional approval. Unconditional acceptance doesn't mean you will approve of everything your spouse may do, nor does it give any of us a free pass on hurtful or damaging behavior.

What it does mean is that you have made up your mind to accept the gift that God has given you in your spouse. You will allow yourself to remember that your spouse was God's answer to your aloneness as a single person however long ago that might have been. And just as God accepts you as you are, you are required to do the same for others.

We did not have to change in order for God to accept us. God is not looking for perfection, He is looking for trust. He accepted us and change occurs based on that unconditional acceptance. This is the best definition of grace: unconditional acceptance. Our unconditional acceptance in Christ is a profound, life-changing truth. The point of the cross is that through Christ's death and resurrection, those who trust in Him become acceptable to God. This did not occur because God decided He could overlook sin. It occurred because Christ paid the penalty for our sins, so He could look beyond our imperfections and present us to the Father—holy, blameless, and beyond reproach.

If we want our marriage to survive and thrive, we must know and accept each other in spite of weaknesses and differences. God's acceptance of us is not based on who we are but on *whose* we are. There is not a more beautiful portrayal of this than God's acceptance of His own child:

"You are my Son, chosen and marked by my love, pride of my life."

—MARK 1:11 (THE MESSAGE)

The Father offered these affirming words of acceptance as Jesus was baptized. This affirmation and acceptance took place before Jesus had even begun His earthly ministry. As far as we know, He had not preached a sermon or performed a miracle, and obviously, He had yet to sacrifice His life. This statement was made by a heavenly Father expressing His acceptance of

60

His Son, not based on what He had done, but based on *whose* He was.

Immediately after this scene of a father's unconditional acceptance, Jesus, while in the wilderness for forty days, was confronted by Satan. One must wonder what part the affirmation He received played in His response to the trials and temptations He endured.

Christians are often hesitant to allow even those closest to them to truly enter their world because of a fear that the *opposite* of grace will happen. It is this fear of being *disgraced* that causes many people to remain closed. No one wants to be rejected. We all fear scathing retribution. We fear being the "only one" who has a problem. This is especially true for ADD individuals who may be doubly guilt-ridden for past mistakes and failures, thinking that everyone else seems to learn from their mistakes, except for them. No one else has problems conforming to rules and procedures or doing the paperwork. Others do not have constant accusations hurled at them, coupled with a truckload of labels, just in case they forget who they are. They know that they are outcasts even in the midst of those who should know them best.

ADD individuals need grace and lots of it. They need the emotional grace that understands and accepts their strengths and weaknesses. If we refuse to offer unconditional acceptance to others, especially our spouse, what does that say about us as Christians, whose faith relies on God's unconditional acceptance of us? What does it signify if we cannot or will not give our acceptance to those who need it the most, those who are closest to us? Let's dare take it a step further: What does it say to our children when we will not accept differences in our spouse, especially to the child who exhibits many of the same ADD characteristics as the ADD parent? It says...

 You must change in order for me to accept you.

- You are defective.

- You are not good enough.

- You are irresponsible.

- You do not make my life pleasant.

- You are not normal.

This part of the blessing of knowing and accepting is what we refer to as the Zacchaeus principle. In the book of Luke we read that while Jesus was visiting a town He took notice of a man (who probably looked something like Danny Devito!) hovering in a tree. Zacchaeus was too short to see over the heads but this didn't keep Jesus from calling him out. In fact, the first thing out of Jesus' mouth is, "Zacchaeus." Jesus *knew* him. He called him by name. Jesus then announced that He was going to his house for dinner. This, in turn, shocked all the religious folks since in that culture it was a sign of acceptance to eat with someone.

We don't have all the details about everything that was said during the dinner at Zacchaeus' house. But we do know a few things that took place: Zacchaeus needed to change his ways and adopt some new behaviors. He needed to fight temptation. He needed a new self-image. He needed to feel valued and accepted. Zacchaeus was *called by name* and *accepted*. Experiencing the blessing caused his heart to turn toward the heavenly Father. He changed, and subsequently his entire household came to know God because of it.

Unconditional acceptance is an attitude—one that must be chosen. You must make the choice to accept your spouse. As you do so, your spouse's heart will be turned toward you *and* God, enabling him or her to overcome trials and temptation and yes, even make some changes.

Love in Action

The next element in this process of blessing is unconditional love. While unconditional acceptance is an attitude, the apostle John tells us that love is more than the words we speak:

Dear children, let us not love with words or tongue but with actions and in truth.
—1 JOHN 3:18 (NIV)

In other words, love is an action—it is something you do. Contrary to what society believes, you measure love by activity, not feelings. Not long ago a good friend of ours called to tell us that she had made the decision to leave her husband. When I questioned her about what went wrong in the relationship, she simply stated that she fell out of love. I tersely informed her that I fall out of love with Phil every Monday, Wednesday, and Friday!

We cannot allow our feelings to dictate whether or not we stay in the covenant of marriage. King David refused to give God an offering that didn't cost him anything! Why did David say this? Because God *gave*.

"I will not sacrifice to the Lord my God burnt offerings that cost me nothing."
—2 SAMUEL 24:24 (NIV)

God gave a precious gift that cost something—a powerful, priceless sacrifice that proved His love for us. Jesus met our ultimate need of salvation by coming into this world and sacrificing His life. He knew the only way to bridge the gap between fallen humanity and a holy God was to lay down His life and die on the cross to pay for our sins. Love is an act of sacrifice. This unmistakable mandate Jesus left us as His legacy requires us to partner in making this kind of love real to our spouse.

Our commitment to each other, to our family, to our friends, and to God should be the sustaining factor through those times

63

when we "fall out of love" with our spouse. Don't allow yourself to become a person who only knows how to "feel" rather than truly love. Anytime you have the opportunity to sacrifice for your spouse, you have the opportunity to show love. The Word says that we should lay down our lives for our brothers, but you and I know it is unlikely that you will be called on to give up your life for anyone in the imminent future. However, you are guaranteed to have to make other sacrifices for them.

The truth is that it doesn't matter how you feel about it; it matters what you *do* about it.

Trust me, Phil did not feel like making the effort to do what he did. What he felt like doing was kicking me in the rear, which is what I deserved!

A couple of years ago, Phil and I were in the process of developing our *Miracle Parenting* course. Because we had originally thought it would take only six to nine months to write the course, we became a little stressed when we came up on the two-year mark. Certain aspects of the project were completed, but as we looked down the hallway of our office, we saw $28,000 worth of books that we couldn't yet market. As the tension mounted, I walked into the office one day and, out of frustration, said something very curt and hurtful to Phil. Not only that, I said it in front of one of our volunteers and Phil's dad! (Further proving that ADD people haven't completely cornered the market on saying the wrong thing at the wrong time!)

I left the office and went home in an effort to calm down. Phil, however, did something very strange. He too left the office but made a forty-five minute drive across town to Sam's Club, where he bought a beautiful bouquet of exotic flowers. He then came home and set the bouquet on our dining room table.

Trust me, Phil did not feel like making the effort to do what he did. What he felt like doing was kicking me in the rear,

64

which is what I deserved! Yet, he knew the Bible says that where his treasure or investment was placed, his heart would follow. When he made that sacrifice, he was assured that his heart would follow. He was investing in me, in our marriage, and in our family. He knew that if he allowed frustrations and hurt to fester, we would enter a danger zone, and that sooner or later we would find ourselves in intensive care, a place where we had been years before and did not want to go again. And as we all know, the biggest problem with being in intensive care is that there are only two ways out: either you get better or you die.

This was where our relationship was headed right about the time we found out that Phil was ADD (remember when Phil started working for someone else?). It had become so painful for both of us that one day he looked at me and said he was about ready to go flip hamburgers on a beach in Florida. I replied that I was about ready to let him! We had a bank account full of negative emotions that had driven us into emotional bankruptcy. We decided at that point to check ourselves into intensive care, with a driving determination not to come out in a body bag.

Did we feel like working on our relationship and facing the wake of damage? No. Did we feel like we loved each other? Absolutely not. Did we feel like we could overcome past mistakes and failures? Not at that time. Did we want to die? No! Did it help to discover an explanation (ADD), a name for what turned out to be the root cause of so many of our struggles? You better believe it did. It gave us a handle of hope to hold onto.

Dealing with ADD in a relationship can still be a challenge even when you have a grip on it. But when ADD is present and it is either unrecognized or unacknowledged, it has the potential to become a nightmare that can lead to hurt, anger, mistrust, or even physical ailments such as headaches, backaches, or depression. Couple that with the normal struggles in a marriage, and you have a perfect recipe for an emotional bankruptcy.

65

During our time in intensive care, Phil and I discovered that not only were we not meeting each other's needs, but we really didn't know what those needs were. In fact, we began realizing that even in our strained efforts to help each other, we were giving each other what we ourselves needed rather than what the other person needed. We realized that in order to become healthy again, we needed to first figure out what our emotional needs were, and then start meeting them for each other.

Our emotional needs help further define love for each of us. They are deep internal longings or desires that, when satisfied, leaves us with a feeling of joy and contentment. When not satisfied we are left with a feeling of despondency, unhappiness, hurt, or anger. Regardless of our age, gender, or status in life, we each have needs.

And my God will meet all your needs according to his glorious riches in Christ Jesus.
—PHILIPPIANS 4:19 (NIV)

We find the first example of man's neediness in Genesis 2. Adam by all accounts had a great life: perfect genetics, pristine environment, and daily devotions with God! While the Creator met his spiritual and physiological needs, God recognized that "it was not good for man to be alone." This proves, as was previously pointed out, that if we reject our spouse then we are actually rejecting God's gift and His answer to our aloneness.

In Eve, God created a companion to help meet Adam's emotional needs. God provided both a horizontal and a vertical means of meeting each of our needs—through Himself and through family, friends, and the church. If you are in the covenant of marriage, then you are the primary horizontal source for meeting the emotional needs of your spouse. It is your calling, your mandate, and a huge part of your purpose in life.

The way you were raised, your culture, your personality, your gender, and your life experiences will help determine your emotional needs. Emotional needs may change with various stages of life, with age, our circumstances, or preferences. Not only do emotional needs apply to every age group, they also transcend cultural, social, and economic differences.

Our Emotional Bank Account

In order to envision how well you may be meeting the emotional needs of your spouse, imagine that every individual has an "emotional bank." Just like your financial bank account, this account can have deposits and withdrawals. This emotional bank account can either be full of positive, healthy, affirming emotions or becomes bankrupt with negative, hurtful, and empty emotions.

A person with a full emotional bank will exhibit traits such as joy, peace, security, and happiness. A person with an empty emotional bank might be angry, depressed, anxious, or even suicidal. If you were to survey people who use drugs, abuse alcohol, or live a destructive lifestyle, you would find that these persons are emotionally bankrupt in some area. This is particularly true for the ADD individual. Somewhere along the way, their emotional needs were unmet. Understanding what our spouse's needs are and learning to meet those needs can mean life or death for them.

The emotional bank cannot be filled with things money can buy. It can only be filled with treasures from your heart— your time, words, and actions. Emotional closeness between spouses is the product of needs being met. When needs are met, the emotional bank account is full of happy, healthy emotions. Needs that go unmet will produce frustration, fear, disappointment, depression, or anger. (Over 90 percent of all anger is a result of hurt, most of the time stemming from unmet needs.)

In order to achieve and maintain this emotional closeness, we need to learn to identify our own priority needs and those

67

of our spouse. Most of us don't have the same needs at the same time. More often than not, we must *ask* our spouse what his or her needs are and how we can meet those needs. The following are the twelve most identified emotional needs. As you read through the list, make a note of your top priority needs and those needs you think your spouse might have.

ACCEPTANCE: *Willingness to receive and acknowledge in a positive manner.* (Romans 15:7)

⊕ **Positive Balance:** A person who feels accepted feels secure, important, valued and confident. He is content and has a sense of belonging to something greater than himself.

⊖ **Negative Balance:** A person who does not feel accepted may feel dejected, insecure, or anxious. He may become disrespectful or unresponsive toward others. He may develop a poor identity or become absorbed in negative influences or behavior.

AFFECTION: *To communicate a tender feeling through physical touch or meaningful words.* (Romans 16:16; 1 Corinthians 16:20)

⊕ **Positive Balance:** People who experience meaningful touch in their lives develop healthy boundaries and a deep sense of security. They know what it is like to feel loved and in turn can love others.

⊖ **Negative Balance:** Lack of affection produces feelings of being alone, abandoned, or unwanted. It may produce feelings of shame or make a person feel devalued. Someone who is not shown affection may be tempted to look for affection in an unhealthy manner or may become withdrawn.

APPRECIATION: *Recognition of the quality, value, or significance of a person; an expression of gratitude.* (1 Corinthians 11:2)

⊕ **Positive Balance:** Those who feel appreciated tend to be positive, optimistic, grateful, and respectful and will have a strong work ethic, coupled with the ability to help and encourage others.

⊖ **Negative Balance:** People who feel unappreciated tend to be pessimistic and easily discouraged. They may feel devalued and worthless, and may also have deep-seated insecurities and self-doubts. They may also become performance-oriented, seeking appreciation they never received.

APPROVAL: *To think or speak well of; to give or have a favorable opinion of.* (Romans 14:18; Mark 10:16)

⊕ **Positive Balance:** People who sense approval feel needed, wanted, and accepted. They will have a stronger confidence in who they are and a secure sense of their identity in Christ.

⊖ **Negative Balance:** People who do not feel approved of may feel shameful or experience unwarranted guilt. They will search out approval or become performance-oriented or workaholics. They may develop a distrust of others, coupled with a deep sense of insecurity and a lack of self-confidence.

ASSURANCE: *Confidence in harmony with relationships; free from fear, harm, or doubt.* (Isaiah 32:17; Colossians 2:2)

⊕ **Positive Balance:** Assured people feel confident in who they are and in who they are becoming. This security can produce a strong faith and deep confidence in God, which results in a giving heart and a grateful, positive perspective on life. They will more easily adapt to situations.

⊖ **Negative Balance:** Insecure people struggle with fear and worry. They may become negative, controlling, or possessive and may also develop an overt sense of self-reliance.

ATTENTION: *To give special consideration by observing or listening; to take notice of or interest in.* (1 Corinthians 12:25; Mark 10:16)

⊕ **Positive Balance:** People who receive attention feel valued and important. Those who are shown interest will develop a willingness to serve and be attentive to others. An inner feeling of self-worth gives them a strong sense of identity.

70

⊖ **Negative Balance:** The most likely result of not receiving attention is seeking it elsewhere. Some may seek out unhealthy attention from others or seek attention through an unhealthy venue such as the Internet. Others may become shy or withdrawn with an underlying sense of worthlessness.

COMFORT: *To strengthen or cheer in time of affliction or distress; to help or give hope in time of grief or pain.* (2 Corinthians 1:3,4)

⊕ **Positive Balance:** People who experience the blessing of comfort will become loving, caring, positive individuals. They will tend to be compassionate and giving, sensitive to the needs of others, and with a strong sense of self-confidence.

⊖ **Negative Balance:** Those who do not experience comfort may exhibit apathy or numbness toward people or situations, and may struggle with understanding or comforting others. They may develop a strong avoidance of emotions or struggle with deep feelings of aloneness and place an emphasis on "fixing situations and people" while seeking to fill the void in their own life.

CONVERSATION: *To attentively listen and engage in meaningful dialogue; to show regard for the thoughts and interests of others; the informal exchange of ideas, thoughts, and interests through spoken words.* (Colossians 4:6; Ephesians 4:29)

⊕ **Positive Balance:** Those who are engaged in conversation feel important, respected, and valued. Conversation allows people to process their inner thoughts and the events of their life. Healthy conversation helps people maintain a clear perspective on life.

71

⊖ **Negative Balance:** People who are not allowed to converse may feel like they have unresolved issues in their life. Developing proper communication or social skills may be a challenge. They may develop difficulties in communicating honestly with themselves or others. They may experience loneliness, frustration, or even depression.

ENCOURAGEMENT: *To give courage, hope, or confidence; to positively urge forward.* (1 Thessalonians 5:11)

⊕ **Positive Balance:** Those who are encouraged will become productive, creative, and positive people with an optimistic attitude. They will have a "can do" attitude.

⊖ **Negative Balance:** Discouraged people tend to be pessimistic, frustrated with life, withdrawn, and negative, and they may lack confidence or have a failure complex.

FORGIVENESS: *To purposefully pardon or relinquish past or present hurts or offenses; to cease feelings of anger or resentfulness.* (Romans 4:7)

⊕ **Positive Balance:** People who experience forgiveness will know how to walk in forgiveness with others. They will have a sense of peace and belonging, and will be capable of developing harmonious relationships.

⊖ **Negative Balance:** Individuals who do not experience forgiveness will carry an intrinsic sense of guilt for past offenses and failures, even at times when they may have done nothing wrong. They may feel alone, embarrassed, and hopeless.

RESPECT: *To feel and show regard, esteem, or concern for; a willingness to show consideration and appreciation toward a person.* (1 Peter 2:17)

⊕ **Positive Balance:** Someone who feels valued is positively assertive while maintaining a sense of compassion, sensitivity, and respect of others. A valued person is loving, eager, and willing to please.

⊖ **Negative Balance:** Those who do not feel valued may develop a "victim" mindset accompanied by feelings of worthlessness or guilt. They may either possess feelings of inferiority or develop a demanding, intolerant persona. They may become detached physically or emotionally from those closest to them.

SUPPORT: *To give aid or encouragement to a person; to assist or help carry a burden or load.* (Galatians 6:2)

⊕ **Positive Balance:** Supported people have hope for the future with a sense of gratefulness. They will develop sensitivity for helping others who are in need.

⊖ **Negative Balance:** People who are not supported will experience a deep fear of failure or weariness toward life. They may become easily discouraged, and feel alone, overwhelmed, or hopeless.

What are your three most important emotional needs? Were you able to identify the priority needs of your spouse? Again, it's best to ask your spouse to go through the list and select his or her own top needs. It is *critical* that you both identify and begin meeting each other's needs.

Phil and I have very different emotional needs and always have had. He can pretty much count on my number one emotional need as always being support. In addition to our four children, I have a ministry that I help direct and manage, a demanding travel schedule, and a sporadic writing schedule. I need to feel that I am supported in my efforts. I can't keep the house clean, cook the meals, do the laundry, help the kids with homework, run the errands, manage the ministry, write this book, and maintain my sanity if I don't have help. I have to enlist the help of my family and, yes, even my ADD husband.

73

Often the ADD spouse needs a lot of acceptance or respect —especially if they are just finding out that they are ADD. I jokingly say that Phil's top three emotional needs are always: affection, affection, and affection!

Can you happen to guess which emotional need is on the bottom of my list? You got it—affection! Honestly, I don't know why this is. I am sure if I spent hundreds of dollars in therapy I would eventually find out that it is probably due to being potty trained at gunpoint or because I was raised near Booger Hollow, Arkansas! Or, it might have something to do with me being slightly impatient, hot natured, and always on the move.

Joking aside, this can be an absolute revelation for couples who have either been giving their spouse what they need instead of meeting each other's priority needs, or not giving anything at all.

I am periodically invited to speak or lead worship at women's conferences. Usually I am away from home for only two or three days at a time. Phil makes good use of this time by doing things with the kids that I have little interest in. They also make the decision, in anticipation of my returning home, to show me how much they love me. Rather than hanging a banner that reads "Welcome Home, Mom," Phil rallies the troops and together they clean the house. Now that is speaking my love language! Phil and the kids are meeting my *big* emotional need of support.

You can be sure that when Phil comes in from a ministry trip, he could care less how high the dishes are piled up, if there is a clean towel in the house, or if he has to shuffle through two feet of grime on the floors. Instead, he's looking for affection. He's not looking for a home-cooked meal. He's looking for affection. In fact, whoever said that the way to a man's heart is through his stomach didn't know my husband. He defines love as affection.

Now if affection is on the bottom of my list and cleanliness is on the bottom of his list, what has to take place in order to meet each other's need? We have to take action and make that sacrifice that we referred to earlier.

It costs Phil nothing to be affectionate with me. That is what he does and who he is. It is very natural for him. But you'd better believe that when he has to unite the kids and clean the house, it requires a huge effort on his part—especially being ADD. It costs him something. It is a sacrifice. It proves his love for me.

I, on the other hand, have to remind myself to hold my husband's hand, give him a quick neck rub, or plan for an evening of intimacy. I have to work at it. I have to think about it. But if it were effortless, then it would not be a sacrifice.

This is how it works in our family: Phil comes in from a trip and because my priority needs have been met, I, in return, am able to meet his needs. I make a deposit in his bank account and he can turn around and make a deposit in my account and in our children's bank account. Our children's account is now full so they can make deposits in each other's accounts or even in our accounts. The family's account is in the black, which paves the way for Phil and I to minister to tens of thousands of people around the world—depositing into their bank accounts.

Consider this scenario:

Two people meet and marry. For the first year they may happily live off "pure emotion." Inevitably the honeymoon wears off and issues float to the surface. They begin "writing checks" from their emotional bank accounts. If each person's emotional bank account is full, they are each able to give out, meeting the other's needs. As additional deposits are made into their emotional banks, their accounts stay in the black.

Unfortunately, this is not usually the way things happen. Most people come into a marriage with an empty emotional bank account. (This explains why 15 percent of all marriages end the first year.) When issues surface, they try to write checks on a depleted account and become emotionally overdrawn. If both came to the marriage with depleted accounts, eventually they go bankrupt.

This understanding of meeting each other's emotional needs was instrumental in getting our marriage out of intensive care. Phil and I now try to practice it every day with each other and with our children. We make a very real effort to stay cognizant of each other's needs. We ask questions, we investigate, and we "search" out. But this is only part of the equation.

Coming to an understanding of meeting emotional needs doesn't always negate the wake of hurt that may have been left behind in a relationship. Phil and I had a bank full of hurts that we had to deal with, knowing instinctively that the hurts would not automatically disappear.

Because of our human nature, it can take a tremendous amount of effort to put aside our pride and ask our spouse the two most difficult, yet critical questions in the English language. These questions have the powerful potential to wipe out the hurt that may have built up in any relationship. The first is:

How have I hurt you?

It is important to hear from our spouse how we may have caused hurt or pain in his or her life. Hearing and acknowledging the offense will enable change to be made in our own life. At this point, it is not important to rebuff the circumstances behind the reason for the hurt. This is not the time to explain why the offense may have happened or deny the charge based on your intentions.

Very few people we know set out to intentionally hurt another person, even in the closest relationships where hurts usually occur. Most hurt is unintentional, and mature Christians must realize that hurt is still hurt. Unintentional hurt still hurts. Even though we did not mean to hurt the other person, it still counts as hurt. "But I didn't mean to" has no place in dealing with hurt and should be replaced with the second critical question:

Will you forgive me?

This question possesses an enormous amount of power. It has the ability to cleanse us from guilt or shame. Someone once said that forgiveness is setting a prisoner free and then realizing the prisoner was you. The choice of forgiveness benefits both parties, removing a blockage in the relationship and setting the stage for healing and positive change to take place. It offers potential for a new future.

Even though learning about Phil's ADD came at a critical time for us and had a profound affect on our relationship, it did not erase our past. It did not automatically remove the emotional baggage or the hurt that had built up. The negative emotions had been allowed to remain for so long that they had

76

come to define who we were. We had forgotten how it felt to be happy, content, and in love. It was for this reason we began having what we call Devotional Time with one another. We believe these appointed times have become a guaranteed weapon in our quest against divisiveness and helped to redefine our relationship.

Devotion: enthusiastic attachment or loyalty to a person or cause

Devotional Time is a preset, determined allocation of time that spouses spend together in open, direct communication on issues affecting their marriage and family. There are three reasons for doing so:

1. This is a time of devoting our hearts and heads to the unity of our marriage. It is during this time where we plan for the future, process the present, and leave our negative past. It is not a time for sexual intimacy, nor is it the same as a date.

2. Devotional Time is a non-threatening way of saying, "We need to talk." It guards against exploding at each other, diminishes bitterness, creates trust and stability, and produces true intimacy.

3. Devotional Time says we care about the stability and perseverance of this marriage enough to carve out time alone. Because we may not always agree, we take this time to ensure that we will not become divided.

Your Devotional Time (or whatever you call your time together) must be given top priority in your relationship. It should come before any outside activities, entertainment, or ministry. It should be held in a place that is conducive to uninterrupted, adult conversation.

Either spouse should feel free to initiate the scheduling of Devotional Times. Non-ADD spouses are usually better suited

77

at recognizing the need for Devotional Time because they tend to be more sensitive to the atmosphere in the home. They are also better at sticking with anything that is routine in nature. It is not the initiating that should matter, but the willingness.

Do not be tempted to minimize the importance of Devotional Time or think you are the exception and don't need it. There are no exceptions, particularly in an ADD marriage. It is imperative to the success of your relationship that you set aside this time with your spouse.

During this time you should discuss things like:

+ Past or present hurts between you and your spouse, whether those hurts were intentional or not

+ What each of your priority needs are and how they can be better met

+ Any emotional needs that are lacking in your relationship, frustrations or stress issues, and issues regarding ADD

+ Issues related to the family as a whole: evaluating priorities, setting goals, planning vacations, etc.

+ Issues regarding the children: emotional needs, discipline, school, relationships

78

Spouses whose marriage is in "maintenance" mode (no serious relational issues or problems) should plan on sitting down together once a week. Never go longer than two weeks at a time without having a Devotional Time—even if it has to take place over the phone or in the car.

Those who find their relationship in crisis may need to enter "intensive care," defined as meeting together on a daily basis until healing and unity is restored. You must understand that even a professional counselor cannot do all it will take to get your relationship back on course. *You* must make the decision that your marriage will stand, and then follow through with actions.

Regardless of whether our marriage is in intensive care or the picture of health, we all must carve out time to maintain and improve our relationship. This is especially true for the ADD marriage.

During these Devotional Times, it is beneficial to get into the habit of using the two most powerful and inspiring relationship statements in the English language:

I love you and I am committed to you.

Tell me more…

These two statements prove your desire to enter your spouse's world, removing that person's potential aloneness. *Tell me more…* communicates that you want to hear what is in the heart of the other person. It denotes concern, a vested interest, and your willingness to listen. It is, indeed, a terrific start in blessing your spouse.

79

Phil grew up in southern California learning to enjoy a number of outdoor sports. One of his favorite hobbies was barefoot water skiing. While learning how to drop the slalom ski, transitioning to feet only, he was taught to look at the horizon where the treetops met the sky. He learned the hard way that when he looked at the water, he would wipe out at forty miles an hour, doing cartwheels across the water.

This is a great life lesson, especially in relationships with a rocky history. *Where you look, you go.* If you focus on the negative in your relationship and what is wrong, then that is where you are going to go. It does little good for any of us to focus on the problem. You know what the problem is. Everyone involved can identify the problem. Instead, we should determine in our heart to center our attention on where we want to go. Focus on solutions rather than problems. The past serves as a mirror as to why you are where you are, but looking back in the rearview mirror will not empower you to stay afloat or go forward.

If you are only now discovering that you or your spouse is ADD, it is important to look for solutions to what you already know are the problems. There are times when my daily mantra is, "What is the solution?"

More often than not, these solutions call for change. Because humans, especially non-ADD people, are creatures of habit, change is not always easy. But neither is the pain of staying where you are. The key is to find what works for your situation.

One of the obvious solutions to an ADD marriage is to work with, rather than against, each other's innate strengths and weaknesses in the context of the relationship. Phil and I sat down during one of our Devotional Times and listed who did what best. Next, we chose those tasks that we preferred over those we hated doing. Once we had our list, we negotiated who did what and how.

> I haven't failed. I've just found 10,000 ways that won't work.
>
> —THOMAS EDISON

For instance, Phil hates cleaning the kitchen, but there are times when he has to do it. It's part of life. When these times occur, we have an understanding that he will clean the kitchen to his maximum ability which is probably going to be around 75 percent of what I consider a clean kitchen. Getting past that percentage becomes much more difficult for him than it would be for the "normal" person. It takes a lot of energy to be something you are not. I recognize this and offer him slack. If the kitchen gets 70–75 percent of the way done, then I am happy. Because we agreed to this arrangement upfront, it diffuses any potential problems.

In addition, Phil may not clean the kitchen in the same way I would. Most women are very particular when it comes to their hair, house, and kids. I remember when our daughters were only three and four years old, and Phil took them on a ministry trip. I was pregnant at the time and appreciated a little break. They were to be gone for only three days, and in preparation for the trip, I fixed each of the girls' hair in pigtails.

Three days later, Dad made it back with the girls in tow and I could tell they had a wonderful time. I did notice that strangely enough the girls' hair was in pigtails. I casually mentioned to Phil that I was impressed that he had figured out how to style their hair. He nonchalantly told me that it was simple: Each night he would loosen the bands so their scalp would not get sore, and the next morning, tighten them. Voila! Even though things may not have been done the way I would have done it or preferred it done, the mission was accomplished. Everyone was happy, including me.

This is a perfect example of allowing ADD individuals to get better at what they are good at instead of harping on them to get better at what they stink at. Phil will never be a good hair stylist. He is good at being a good father. This applies to every arena of an ADD person's life whether helping out around the house, dealing with kids, career, or ministry. Allowing those who are ADD to focus on improving their strengths will set them up for success rather than failure.

We should note here that when evaluating who does what, it is important to identify the most problematic areas first. For instance, if the biggest frustration in your marriage is finances (which tends to be true in relationships where ADD is undiscovered or is not acknowledged), then put that on the top of the list to fix. You may find yourself in your financial situation due to frequent job changes, abusing credit, gambling, or impulsive purchases. Whatever the cause, use direct and sensitive communication during your Devotional Time to find a solution to your financial problems. (Caution: Nine times out of ten, the ADDer's solution will be to make more money!)

There is not a doubt that the ADD person can make money and a lot of it. The challenge comes with managing the money.

Phil has always done well earning an income because of his entrepreneurial spirit, his knowledge of how the market works, and his pure determination. His challenge is impulse spending. This is especially difficult for him to control during down times or when he had just completed a big project or returned home from a trip. For example, there were times when he needed a new suit, but instead of going and getting one suit, he would come home with three new suits. Of course this was pre-ADD days and we have since put into place a system of accountability.

If Phil is going to spend over a certain amount of money, he talks to me about it first. After we discovered he was ADD, we put this into practice immediately. At that time, the limit we decided on was $100. Since then, he has learned to consider purchases for twenty-four hours, taking me with him when making large purchases (or at least keeping his cell phone handy in order to discuss it with me), and not carrying an excessive amount of cash with him.

I don't particularly care for managing finances, and this is one area in which we had to evaluate and make changes because our finances were in a mess. We decided that, in addition to the above changes, Phil would try to continue in this role. We immediately signed up for online banking where Phil can see the exact balance and all the account activity. Most of our bills are now paid online while others are assigned to our bookkeeper to pay. These minor changes have made an enormous difference in our finances and in the amount of stress that always seemed to lurk in this area.

As we continued in our process of evaluation and negotiation, we recognized that many of our task preferences and abilities didn't necessarily line up with mainstream marriages. For instance, I don't cook. I never have and never will. In my opinion, kitchens in homes are for resale value only! Phil, on the other hand, enjoys cooking and is very good at it. So our agreement is that when he cooks, I clean.

Phil does the laundry and I clean the garage. He buys the groceries, I put them away. Our four children go to four different schools. He deals with everything regarding the daughter in college and the son in private school. I deal with everything regarding the daughter and son who attend public schools.

Strange as it may seem, we have found what works for our family, and you need to do the same.

A great piece of advice Phil's father gave him (even before we knew Phil was ADD) was to "hire out his weaknesses." While Phil doesn't exactly "hire" me, we do work well together, finding a balance of what works not only in our marriage relationship, but in our ministry endeavors.

People who are ADD often see twenty years down the road. They get the big picture. They are the idea people, the visionaries, and the ones who initiate change. Especially in a fluid ministry such as ours, this can be great unless you have a staff member who has panic attacks every time the office gets moved around!

We have to make sure that our staff understand that Phil thinks out loud. If, out of left field, Phil says he would like to move the office around, what he is really saying is that he is *thinking* about moving the office around. He is brainstorming without a time frame. The thought that is in his brain comes out of his mouth—even though we may have just moved the office around the month before.

If Phil comes up with a new project, as he so brilliantly does, then we as a team consider the new endeavor. Who is going to take the project from point A to point B? Who is capable and who is willing? An ADD person has about a three- to six-month attention span on most projects, so who will make sure it is completed if it requires prolongation? These and other questions must be asked when considering major commitments. Remember, the ADDer is the idea person, but someone has to do the follow-through. I often say that Phil is great at

83

buying cows, but stinks at milking them! If left to milk cows, either he will try to invent a faster way to do it or he will become bored and the cows will explode.

Understanding Your Limitations

Our expectations and solutions have to be realistic. This is why it is so important to understand the limitations that can occur in the everyday life of the ADD individual. The young fire chief we mentioned at the beginning of the book was officially diagnosed as having ADD. After going through a battery of tests, his doctor gave him a telling example of how he functioned. She related to him that if he were sent to the grocery store to buy three items, he functioned at the level of someone who had a master's degree. If, however, only one additional item was added to the request, his functionality dropped to a fifth-grade level.

Once we found out that Phil was ADD, we informed all of our close friends and family in order to enlist their support. At that time, we didn't know exactly what we were dealing with, but we had enough information to help those who loved Phil understand him much better. Everyone seemed relieved that there was, indeed, an explanation to so many unanswered questions and genuine concerns.

Our life has been far from perfect since the discovery of this newfound explanation called ADD. The better way to describe our life post-ADD is that it has become more "normal." Still there are days when Phil becomes paralyzed because of ADD. Stress can exacerbate ADD symptoms making it difficult for the ADD individual to function on all eight cylinders. This can be even more problematic if the ADDer has not experienced any down time or, as we say, "crash days." After big events, projects, or working nonstop for an extended period, ADD individuals need to crash. The harder they fight it, the worse it gets. They need to be allowed to do whatever helps them crash. For some, it may be sleeping. For others, it might be playing video games, going to the movies, or playing golf. Both the ADDer and the non-ADD person will be better off accepting this as fact, taking some time off, and hitting it hard the next day or so.

Phil still struggles with certain aspects of ADD and probably always will. He has, however, enlisted my help especially in social situations. We have arranged signals to bring to his attention that he is interrupting people or needing to be more aware of a person or the conversation taking place.

ADD can be accompanied by learning disabilities—not always, but often. In Phil's case, he has a minor form of dyslexia, which mainly shows up in his spelling and reading abilities. We also noticed that after a long day of ministry, Phil's eyes tend to drift downward during conversations. We have yet to find out if this is due to the dyslexia or the problem he had as a child with peripheral vision. This became one area where we had to create a signal because as Phil would be involved in a conversation following a time of ministry, his eyes would begin to focus around chest level. Not a huge problem if he is talking to a man! With a signal, he now knows he must make a conscientious effort to maintain eye contact at all times.

Arranging signals, discussing issues during Devotional Times, and lightening up on some issues can remove so much of the tension, embarrassment, and frustration that can occur in an ADD marriage. It takes a little time and effort, but will definitely pay off in the long run.

Another problematic area for the ADD marriage can be what takes place in the bedroom or perhaps what doesn't take place. Sex can easily become a source of contention that often leads to emotional separation. Trust, intimacy, and excitement can be brought back into the bedroom with a little understanding of what might be going on in the mind of the ADD spouse.

Phil and I once heard a story about a husband who desired to put a little more spice in his and his wife's sex life. Deciding

85

to play along, the wife let her husband tie her to the bedpost after which he donned a full Batman costume. In his effort to stage a "rescue," the man climbed onto a chest of drawers and proceeded to jump off. Unfortunately, Batman jumped a little too high, hit the ceiling fan and was knocked out cold. The wife had no recourse but to scream for several hours before the neighbors called the police. The man ended up with a slight concussion, the police enjoyed a good laugh, and Phil and I inherited a great ADD story.

Sex is important in any marriage and has the potential to be a serious source of unnecessary strife, particularly in the ADD marriage. By focusing on real solutions rather than on the problem, sex in an ADD marriage can be passionate and exciting.

One of the first things that must be dealt with is to ensure all unresolved conflict gets taken care of. If you skipped to this part first and missed the earlier section on meeting emotional needs, then go back and make sure you understand what your spouse really needs from you first—before sex.

Please allow me to go ahead and get two general thoughts on sex out of the way:

1. Most women have a difficult time focusing on or desiring sex when their life is not in order (e.g., a dirty house, piles of laundry, unhappy kids, unmet emotional needs).

Men, the quicker you learn this, the more sex you will get.

2. Most men have a difficult time focusing on anything if they are not getting enough sex. Plus, lack of sex makes men cranky.

Women, the quicker you learn this, the more help you will get around the house.

It would be nice to stop there, but in our experience in dealing with ADD, we have found it to be a little more complicated than that. For starters, ADD individuals tend to either be

86

able to hyper-focus on sex with no attention deficit anywhere in sight or they have difficulty staying focused when sex is the only distraction.

There are those ADD individuals who have an inordinate desire for sex. They always have had and probably always will. They can't get enough. Their ability to hyper-focus allows them to maintain an interest for hours on end.

This can become a problem when one spouse desires a lot of sex while the other is not anywhere on the same page. The more desirous spouse may feel rejected, hurt, or angry if his sexual needs go unmet. The spouse who has less of a desire may feel pressured or guilty for not being able or willing to meet the needs of her spouse.

Not only can the more desirous spouse not get enough, he may have a tendency to crave more novel types of sex due to becoming bored with the same Friday night routine in the same missionary position. It is helpful to remember that the ADD individual naturally craves stimulation and enjoys variety. Sex can and should be fun and creative.

87

There are those ADD individuals who may have little desire for sex or may have a desire, but know by experience that they may have difficulty staying focused during the act. They may struggle to keep their mind from wandering off or become easily distracted by something as simple as the air conditioner coming on. This may lead to embarrassment on the part of the ADD spouse and frustration on both parts. Again, communication is the key and it is important to remain solution-oriented without being judgmental or degrading. Be creative and find what works for your situation.

Most couples don't communicate enough at all, much less talk about what they enjoy or desire regarding sex. This is a good topic for your Devotional Time. For some, it might be a simple matter of scheduling when and how sex takes place. This may sound sterile or cold-hearted, but it actually can work.

Putting a night of intimacy on the calendar enables both of you to get prepared in all areas. It also allows more non-sexual intimacy on "off nights." Particularly the less desirous, less affectionate spouse becomes more open to snuggling or back rubs on the off night knowing it will not lead to sex. On the scheduled night, both have worked to make sure those things that can cause distractions are eliminated or at least minimized.

Keeping the lines of communication open diffuses most problems in the area of sex. Failing to honestly and directly communicate can set the stage for the spouse who feels ignored sexually to become deceitful about sexual behavior. This may reveal itself in actual affairs, emotional affairs, or through more accessible means such as the Internet.

We don't want to see any couple get to the point in their relationship where the only recourse is prayer. This is not how God designed the covenant of marriage to operate.

If you are not doing your part, then do what it takes to figure out why, whether due to unmet emotional needs, unresolved conflict, or perhaps a medical problem. Stay determined to find a solution.

We don't want to see any couple get to the point in their relationship where the only recourse is prayer. This is not how God designed the covenant of marriage to operate. Knowledge is power and its effect on the ADD marriage should not be diminished. Some adults with ADD (particularly men) will refuse to accept help even when confronted with a "name" or explanation for all the unexplainable missed opportunities, accusations, failures, and disappointments. Even so, the non-ADD spouse must become educated and remain supportive. And it is worth repeating that I have found it even more important that the non-ADD spouse have a greater understanding of ADD than the ADD individual.

Of course, there is the flip side of the coin where the ADD adult uses the ADD as an excuse—blaming his messiness, rudeness, and impulsiveness on his newfound explanation. This may be understood on occasion but should not become a permanent crutch. There are days when Phil looks at me and says, "ADD is kicking my rear today." I back off and give him some slack. But it is certainly the exception rather than the rule.

Look for the good in the ADD person. Allow yourself to see the creativity, loyalty, charisma, kindness, and compassion that may have been buried due to years of misunderstanding. These traits are there though they may have to be rediscovered.

In our parenting seminars, Phil and I challenge parents to catch their children doing something *right*. The same should apply to our spouse. I'm thankful that Phil does so many things right as a father, a husband, and an advocate for families all over the world. Yet I note that it is so easy to allow the hiccups in our lives to overshadow the good that takes place every day. Inevitably we all fall short of the mark. We need to offer each other more slack and more grace. In so many ways, we need to lighten up on each other, work to protect each other's self-image (who we are in Christ), and watch the back of those closest to us. It doesn't mean life or our marriage will ever be perfect, but each of us can focus on what is missing in our life, or be content and grateful with what we have.

Have you ever really wondered what makes a cow stick its neck through a barbed wire fence to chew grass on the other side? It's a strange thing to watch. Usually the grass is the exact same on both sides of the fence. Yet the cow is convinced that the grass is greener on the other side. The cow is not content with where it is and what it has.

Lack of contentment in a marriage relationship breeds ugly thoughts. If left unchecked, it becomes easy to begin thinking stupid thoughts, which leads to doing stupid things. Over 60 percent of second marriages fail. Why? Same song, second verse.

89

Same baggage and the same refusal to accept a person for who he is and allow God to change him. Do not be fooled: the grass is not always greener on the other side.

The last line of defense for so many ADD individuals is, *I don't know.* I don't know why I say the things I do or why I do the things I do. Most ADDers can completely relate to Paul's struggle:

> *I do not understand my own actions. For I do not do what I want, but I do the very thing I hate.*
> —ROMANS 7:15 (RSV)

As the most important person in the life of an ADD spouse, now you *do know.* One of the most vital missions you have is to help give the ADD person back his passion and purpose in life. And at the risk of sounding curt, his purpose in life is not to make your life more pleasant. The greater picture, the eternal picture is so much bigger than that.

Peter, the guy in the New Testament who at times acted as though he had no filter in his brain, was consistently doing and saying things without thinking. I do not doubt that Peter, the ADD disciple, wrote the following scripture out of his own need:

> *And above all things have fervent love for one another, for love will cover a multitude of sins.*
> —1 PETER 4:8

We get one shot at this life. We can make it about us or we can make it about others. We can choose to be right or we can choose to be content. One thing is for sure: it *is* a choice.

CHAPTER FOUR

Racing Among Workhorses

"Some people see things as they are and ask, Why?
Others see things as they could be and ask, Why not?"
—FRANKLIN D. ROOSEVELT

FORMER CO-WORKER (ANONYMOUS BY REQUEST)

Our church was excited to learn that Phil would come and work as part of our pastoral staff. For years our pastor had respected Phil's ministry and often asked him to fill the pulpit in his absence. It was a double treat to get Cynthia along with him. Everyone noticed that they were both talented, hardworking, caring individuals with a passion and vision for helping families.

For a while, all seemed well. Our church enjoyed having a noted, successful specialist like Phil on our staff. However, in my opinion and hindsight as a fellow staff member, our pastor may have thought he was hiring one type of person and what he got was something totally different.

After a couple of years or so of working with Phil, one of the other staff members commented to Cynthia that he didn't understand why Phil interrupted him and others in our weekly staff meeting. He went on to say that Phil was arrogant, rude, and insensitive. Because I worked closely with Phil, I knew firsthand that he was smart, gifted, talented and, yes, even sensitive. Phil was a great visionary. He just didn't fit our mold.

Compared to the other staff members, Phil's office was a complete mess with dozens of piles everywhere. He was always studying several books at once, while listening to music and working on the computer. Phil was usually on the cutting edge as far as technology was concerned. It was in the early '90s during one of our staff meetings when Phil brought up the idea of our church needing a website. We all just sat there and gave him that "calf at a new gate" look.

Phil was motivated and genuinely cared about the people in our church. He was known as the approachable pastor. He and Cynthia worked great as a team and seemed to balance each other out. They were some of the most productive and effective pastors I have ever known.

To this day, I have difficulty putting my finger on what went wrong, if anything. Phil just did not seem to fit in. Cynthia understood office policies, and even staff politics, if you will. Phil was unintentionally intimidating to the other pastors on staff. He and Cynthia put in long hours, were loved by the people, had good ideas, and were progressive in their thoughts, ideas, and actions.

I didn't know a lot about ADD back then, but I did feel as though I knew Phil. I didn't think of him as being arrogant or cocky. In fact, it was his progressiveness, his boldness, his natural resistance at being a "yes man" that earned my deep respect and sense of awe and envy.

After Phil received an official diagnosis of having Attention Deficit Disorder, I remember a guest evangelist giving a "word" in front of the entire congregation that Phil would be healed of his brain disorder. I sat there thinking, *Wow, we should all be so sick.*

Sometime ago, when Phil and I were driving through the back roads of Pennsylvania, we noticed an Amish farmer beautifully handling a team of plowhorses. It presented an incredible picture with eight of the most superb animals we have ever seen, all working in a regimented concert. The farmer masterfully directed their deliberate and ordered steps. Their massive beauty spoke of hundreds of years of breeding in order to become great assets to the farmers who owned them.

The racehorse is also a magnificently bred animal—well cared for, meticulously trained, and remarkable to watch. Bred and trained to race, the racehorse's workday could be measured in seconds. Racing is what they have been conditioned to do. It is what they are built for. It is why racehorse owners spend millions of dollars to breed these animals. When the starting gate opens, the only thing on the mind of a racehorse is to run as fast as possible around the track. Once the race is over, it is over. The job is done.

If one were to attach to a team of plowhorses an exceptionally bred racehorse, it is without a doubt that chaos would break out. Why? The racehorse would try to do what he was wired to do: race. The entire team would be confused, frustrated, and out of kilter. The racehorse is not geared to work with a team of other horses. Plowhorses are slow and methodical. They are trained to till: to do the same thing day in and day out. They use a different set of muscles than the racehorse. They think differently for a different purpose. They become distracted only if their routine is imposed upon. There is no need to look for ways to speed up their job. No competent horse trainer would ever attempt to race a workhorse. The plowhorse would be completely incapable of performing the job of a racehorse. And vice versa.

In so many ways, this illustration represents the life of an ADD individual. Wired to race, to react and think quickly, they are the racehorse removed from the track and expected to function in all areas of society as a workhorse. Unrealistic or unguided expectations at home, work, school, and even church create frustration while setting up the ADD individual for failure, wreaking potential havoc in virtually every area of his life. Just as the racehorse and the workhorse function differently and for different reasons, so do those who are ADD and those who are not. Both the racehorse and workhorse have a purpose and a value. One is not better than the other, only very different.

Just as the racehorse and the workhorse function differently and for different reasons, so do those who are ADD and those who are not.

94

Is it possible that the difference in the way ADD people function in our society has become such a matter of intolerance and misunderstanding that we have acquiesced by labeling them as having a disorder? Have we come to the place where we believe there are only normal people and sick people, with no allowance for differences?

The only time you find one kind of grass on this earth is when man had something to do with it. God created differences in not only nature, but in each of us in order to keep our lives playing in living color. Some of us were created to prefer order, routine, and calm. Others are wired to take risks, to invent, and to visualize the future. If we deny acceptance of those who are different than ourselves, we have denied a foundational element on which our faith is built.

Considering our own nation's history, it is not surprising that there is a much larger percentage of those who have ADD characteristics in the United States than in countries such as Japan or China. Just as the history of an ADD person tells much, so does the history of our nation and of the Americas in general.

Two Basic Personalities

Our family had the opportunity to live in Costa Rica for a couple of years. During this time we became close friends with a man named Juan Carlos Esquivel. In one of our many conversations, we asked him how his family came to live in one of the most beautiful countries in the world. He related the story that had been passed down from generation to generation of how his great, great, great grandfather, a count, left his castle in Spain, foregoing his wealth and belongings. He then set sail on an adventure that would land him on the shores of Costa Rica. Upon venturing deep into the sparsely populated, unspoiled jungle, Count Esquivel simply decided it was a good place to live.

95

One must wonder what kind of person would leave his castle to live in a virtually uninhabited jungle? Who willingly exchanges comfort and safety for unknown and life-threatening conditions? Not many!

Hundreds of years before the count arrived in Costa Rica, another man who personified courage, resilience, and confidence arrived in Limon, Costa Rica. Christopher Columbus led a charge for change while paving the way for additional explorers and risktakers to venture across the seas. Those voyagers envisioned a new world and a new way of doing things. Their techno-colored dreams would make history and change the world.

Add this new blood to the human landscape of millions of Native Americans already here, and the country got one power-punched mix of people. They were hunters in search of a new life, land, and food. And it would be these hunter-type personalities who constituted the original makeup of our country.

One of the most interesting theories regarding ADD and genetic differences recognizes that historically there have been basically two types of societies since the creation of the world: a farming society and a hunting society. During the worldwide Agriculture Revolution, farming became more efficient than hunting in providing sustenance and as a means of survival. This would create a movement where farmers would begin to outnumber hunters.

In our own country, the transition to a more farmer-based society became particularly evident during the Industrial Revolution where hunter traits became more of a disadvantage than an advantage. Part of this change would stem from the influx of Irish farmers who came to this country because of the potato famine. When their own farms ceased to work, they were forced to change. They had to make the trip to America and, once here, many went no farther than the east coast. Circumstances, rather than a desire for adventure or change, forced the farmers to take risks.

This change from hunting for survival to the new nineteenth-century farm and manufacturing plant would alter the face of our nation. A more scheduled, focused, and regimented way of life became more valued and more popularly practiced. The farmer systematically tilled the soil, planted the seed, cared for and waited for its growth, and later harvested the crop. It required planning, patience, persistence, and a linear sense of time. There was no room or tolerance for a risk-taking entity on the farm; rather it required a careful, patient, and organized approach. Farmers needed everything to function the same way it functioned the day before. They counted on it and depended on a routine.

Likewise, the factory worker possessed many of these same traits. Routine, steadfastness, and order were the determining factors in the success of a factory. Newly established methods and systems were reinforced by policies and correct procedures.

96

Workdays were defined by days and set hours. These farmer-type personalities were capable of doing the same task over and over again, maintaining a "shoulder to the wheel" kind of focus. Their day was over when the whistle was blown, but only to return the next day, and the next to repeat the process.

Today, there remain those who naturally function better in a more routine and structured environment. They are the accountants, bankers, assembly workers, and the like who easily comply with, and prefer a kind of, gauged surrounding. And often, looking back at one's lineage explains the predisposition to this kind of lifestyle.

The same often holds true for ADD individuals who exhibit the hunter-type personality. Usually, a glance at their ancestry would prove they indeed inherited the characteristics associated with ADD. The need for stimulation, change, and new endeavors might represent those today who are salesmen, inventors, artists, entrepreneurs, firemen, policemen, or mechanics.

It's not that ADD individuals despise routine and order. In fact, routine is good for ADDers. It is more an issue of not being able to stick with the routine. ADDers don't excel in planning. They pride themselves on figuring things out as they go. They excel in emergencies enabling them to make quick decisions. There is no routine or right way of doing things. They act first, and ask questions later. Their personal philosophy might be: It's better to ask forgiveness than permission. Their hunt is a big project or a potential sale. They may chart out new territory in their hunt and once the sale is closed, the fire is put out, or the project is completed, they celebrate their kill. The hunt is over. The race is won. And more times than not, after the kill, the ADDer comes in from the hunt and crashes.

In observing our society today, the makeup looks something like the following: Around 20 percent of the population would strongly identify with the adventurous, impulsive hunter-type persona, 20 percent with the routine, organized farmer-type,

97

with the remaining 60 percent or so somewhere in the middle. We respectfully refer to those in the middle as ranchers.

The majority of people we know are ranchers, who enjoy a little adventure here and there and are also capable of maintaining a semblance of routine. They are not extreme either way. They are flexible, but appreciate structure. They can be impulsive but are not driven by a need for stimulation. Their lives are not easily dictated by risk, adventure or change, nor by systematic schedules and routine.

The biggest problem people with ADD face each and every day is that they live in what has become a society geared to timeliness, structure, routine, and organization. Consider how many people have the following schedule: go to work Monday through Friday, 8 A.M. to 5 P.M., go out to eat Friday night, do yard work and clean the house on Saturday, go to church or recreate on Sunday, and start the entire cycle again on Monday.

The same challenge applies to children who are ADD. Regardless of whether they are wired to race, they are required to endure endless hours and days of tilling—sitting in school desks day after day (now more than ever in the history of our country) and expected to learn in a standardized linear manner. The ADD child faces the same challenge as the ADD adult: surviving in a concrete jungle. The only difference is that the ADD adult now knows what is at stake.

ADD individuals who understand their strengths and weaknesses can bring tremendous insight, creativity, and ingeniousness to any business or career. They are the visionaries, often seeing years down the road and able to easily grasp the big picture. ADDers can be good at making money. Their high energy, risk-taking, and creative tendencies can all translate into profitable productivity. Again, it is usually the managing of the money that becomes a challenge.

Career choice is critical for those who are ADD. We have seen way too many ADDers in the wrong profession. Others have changed jobs so many times that those closest to them end up in a perpetual state of aggravation. For so many ADD individuals, life is all about getting around the track, regardless of how it's done. They are simply looking for a way to make it. It is difficult for them to face jobs that require efficiency, organization, and promptness as most jobs do. And in the mind of an ADD individual, office policies and procedures have one goal —to harness the racehorse to a plow and make him turn out the results. It can be very difficult, but not at all impossible, for ADD adults to find their niche and make a living at it.

Often an ADD individual finds himself in a career that was chosen for him or handed down to him. We witnessed this not too long ago when, after one of our seminars on ADD, a young man came up to us in tears. He related how he inherited an accounting business from his father, who had previously inherited it from his father. Of course accounting is very tedious, regimented, and involves much paperwork. The young man went on to say how much he dreaded going to work and how he hated every minute of it once there. He was a square peg trying to force himself into a round hole. He was miserable and on his way to burning out. He was a fenced-in racehorse expected to do the job of a workhorse.

In the right situation, an ADD individual can be tremendously successful. Great minds such as the Wright Brothers, Albert Einstein, Sir Winston Churchill, Leonardo da Vinci, Walt Disney, Thomas Edison, and Malcolm Forbes all had characteristics of being ADD.

Those with these ADD-type minds are often brilliant and convincing in their arguments. They make great trial lawyers, politicians, or evangelists. They are the policeman, the emergency room doctor, the pilot, the inventor, and the successful entrepreneur. And the one thing they all have in common is a drive for the adventure aspect of their job and a dread for the follow-up or the constraint of sitting behind a desk.

99

The ADD mechanic welcomes the challenge of a problematic car, but considers it an intrusion to stop and fill out the report. The car salesman is thoroughly persuasive and actually enjoys the challenge of closing a sale, but the paperwork required after the sale drives the ADDer crazy.

The ADD pastor enjoys preparing for Sunday morning messages (since each Sunday morning is like a hunt). It is usually the other duties that weigh him down. He dislikes tedious board meetings and he struggles with making or keeping appointments or even remembering people's names. In addition, those in ministry (and who should know better than anyone) are often the worst at admitting that the Kingdom of God will not fall apart if they take a real day off. Understanding all of the above can prevent burnout on the part of the ADD pastor or other spiritual leader.

A wise employer will make an effort to become educated on ADD and offer some understanding and flexibility on behalf of the ADDer.

100

With an ADD person on staff, the employer will never be stuck in a rut. A wise employer will make an effort to become educated on ADD and offer some understanding and flexibility on behalf of the ADDer. The workplace can greatly benefit from these energetic, intelligent, and loyal individuals. The ADD person should be set free to do what he does best—talk, sell, troubleshoot, argue, plan, dream, or whatever it may be. Then, the employer should hire around the weaknesses of the ADDer by finding those who, if you will pardon the expression, can get the grunt work done.

We do this in our own organization by making sure that the majority of people we hire are more farmer-type oriented. Between Phil, his dad, and a couple of staff members, we have enough visionaries. What we look for are people who can put legs on all the different projects we have going on. We also make a concerted effort to place those who come to work for us in their areas of strength, regardless of what our need might be at that time.

ADD in the Workplace

Employees of an ADD person need to be flexible and expect frequent change. In our organization, we make sure that those who will work with Phil understand that he thinks and processes things out loud. He may come in and announce that it would be good to rebuild our website, but until the time comes when either he starts making changes or issues a direct request to do so, it may not ever take place. It was just a thought, something that may or may not happen. Employees also need to understand that, at times, the ADD boss can say things without thinking or even do things without thinking, while leaving the employee to "clean up the mess."

101

It is wise for the ADD boss to first discuss new projects with those who will have direct responsibility for the follow-through, especially when working with a spouse. Phil does not begin any new projects unless he has first talked with those who work with him—especially me. Again, he is great at buying cows, but someone has to milk them.

A couple of years ago our staff fell into a habit of giving Phil his phone messages on Post-It notes. I would walk into his office and he would have dozens of small notes stuck to his door, his chair, and on his desk. I recognized that this was a very dangerous way of giving an ADDer his messages, so we found a computerized phone message system. Phil now gets a hardcopy of the phone message handed to him, emailed to him, and then kept in the archives of the computer program. There are plenty of practical solutions such as this that the ADDer can implement to help organize his life. Not all will work for every individual, but the key is to find what works for him and then for him to do it.

Many look at Phil and cannot understand that he is ADD—especially while observing him in a speaking engagement. Though he teaches without notes, he is always well organized and he never loses his train of thought. And, unlike some non-ADD preachers, he ends on time! After hearing Phil speak, it is not surprising to have someone (at times even a medical professional) come up to us and ask how Phil could be ADD when he seems so focused, systematic, and organized.

What they do not realize is that when Phil stands in front of a crowd, he is in the heat of a race. There is no attention deficit while running the race and a finish line is within his sight. He is at full attention, fully capable of holding crowds captive and can teach for three, four hours at a time for days on end, if need be. There is no deficit and certainly no brain disorder in play as Phil travels often to some of the hardest-to-reach places in the world. There may be an occasional lost passport or missed train, but all in all, I refer to him as "the Hummer" on these difficult trips. He is built for adventure and problem solving and does it well.

However, there is one thing that both the ADD individual and the non-ADD person must understand: the inevitable ADD crash. When Phil returns home after a ministry engagement, whether a three-day event or a month-long journey to a foreign country, he crashes. The longer and more difficult the trip, the harder the crash. There is no denying it. The harder he fights against it or the harder I challenge him to keep from crashing, the more paralyzed he will become.

This became a problem for a youth pastor we knew who almost lost his job, because neither he nor his senior pastor knew he was ADD. The senior pastor was constantly frustrated when the youth pastor would show up late or miss staff meetings entirely. When he did make it, he seemed unable to focus and unwilling to contribute. This did not at all portray the success he was having with his youth program. In fact, when we

102

asked the senior pastor if he thought his youth pastor was doing a good job with the youth, he unequivocally replied that he was very happy with his accomplishments but just wished that he would be more of a team player during staff meetings.

We subsequently discovered that the youth had their big event of the week on Wednesday nights and that the staff meeting was held each Thursday morning. It was obvious that the ADD youth pastor was experiencing post-event crashing on Thursdays. We recommended that either the youth pastor be given Thursdays off or the staff meeting be moved to a different day. They took our recommendation and did both, which saved a working relationship and possibly deflected a lot of unnecessary hurt and confusion.

More cars will be sold, more fires put out, better sermons will be preached, and more projects will be completed if we will learn the art of working with each other's strengths and weaknesses in a society of diversity. It will benefit all of us to remember that a racehorse works best with short-term projects, thrives on change, and needs a stimulating challenge. This is the way they were created. They will never become plowhorses unless beaten into compliance. Nobody would dispute the value of the plowhorse to the farmer or the racehorse to the owner. It is only when we try to make all horses perform the same, regardless of their uniqueness, that problems arise.

Not only does this happen in the workplace, it occurs in what should be the most accepting and understanding place in all of society: the church. Often those who are ADD are so severely misunderstood, labeled as backslidden or are seen as lacking in spiritual maturity, that irreparable damage takes place, thus alienating many from church. If it is true that 20–30 percent of our society has ADD characteristics, yet as the church (Christian spouses, parents, employers, teachers), we fail to capture their hearts, then we are fighting our battle to fulfill the Great Commission with less than a third of our potential forces.

103

As Christians, we cannot afford to lose this group of natural frontline soldiers. If you were the enemy, trying to defeat the church, where would your first line of attack be? It would begin with those who are the most exposed, the risk-taking warriors— whether the eight-year-old boy or the forty-eight-year-old man.

Accepting the Differences

Our young fire chief and his wife did not make it. Although he was more than willing to work on the marriage, his wife could not get past her false notion that he was not a godly man. She filed for divorce even in the face of real answers to most of their problems. She refused to accept that he was different in every way, including the way he worshiped God. After all, she woke each morning at the same time, fixed a cup of chamomile tea and sat with a devotional book, not understanding why her husband did not practice this spiritual discipline in the same way she did. Though he read the Bible—in his own way, in his own time—she believed her husband to be spiritually deficient.

104

Women often expect men to have the same kind of relationship with God that they do. It only exacerbates the last thirty-something years of attempting to feminize our men even within the confines of the church. We need to allow men the freedom of having a masculine relationship with God. Spiritual discipline should be defined as doing whatever brings you closer to God.

> *There has got abroad a notion, somehow, that if you become a Christian you must sink your manliness and turn milksop.*
> —CHARLES SPURGEON

When Phil and I were first married, we attended a large church known for its prayer ministry. The church held prayer services each morning at 5 A.M. I always wondered why Phil never sat or knelt while praying, but paced in the back of the sanctuary. He was the only person I remember seeing do that, but I wonder now how many would have been more comfortable worshipping God in a manner more suited to how God created them. What about individuals, like Phil, who must move about when they pray or who prefer listening to an audio Bible because of difficulty in reading it? What of the person who spends his alone time with God in a car rather than in the prayer closet? Who is to say which is normal? Certainly the Bible does not.

Our spiritual disciplines are only that—spiritual disciplines. Many of the spiritual disciplines we practice today cannot be found in the Bible, yet they are preached as if they were biblical commands. And in truth, many are prototypes developed by farmer-type personalities because they work for them! One should read so many chapters a day from the Bible to reach spiritual maturity, or pray so many hours a day at a certain time of day and in a certain position. There is little biblical precedence for what are sometimes taught as biblical absolutes.

105

Biblical absolutes are non-negotiable foundations of our faith. They do not change. They are the concrete terms that define our salvation. Some biblical absolutes would include that Jesus was born to a virgin, Jesus is the Son of God, and Jesus died for our sins and was resurrected. It is only through our faith and trust in Him that we are offered eternal salvation. These absolutes are not up for argument or negotiation.

Convictions are what the Holy Spirit places in each of us to guide us and bring us into full maturity in Him. The Holy Spirit may convict you to homeschool your child, fast once a week, give money to an orphanage, or to pray each morning at 5 A.M.

There are *personal preferences* that enable each of us to live life in color. You may prefer to dress more formally for church while others feel more comfortable in casual dress. Some prefer contemporary Christian music while others prefer hymns. These personal preferences can extend beyond spiritual disciplines into all areas of our lives. For example, you may prefer to drive a European car, while others prefer American cars. I like my husband with a scruffy beard. Other women prefer a clean-shaven look. It is important to understand the difference among biblical absolutes, convictions, and personal preferences.

When we teach preferences or convictions as biblical absolutes, people get confused and hurt. They walk away from church having been shot by friendly fire. Many of the injured are those we so easily define by their unorthodox ways, their seeming lack of spiritual depth, and their struggle with normalcy. They are the ones who are Affectionately Designed Differently. They don't belong or fit our nice ordered milieu. We wounded them and didn't even need the help of the enemy to do it.

Welcome with open arms fellow believers who don't see things the way you do. And don't jump all over them every time they do or say something you don't agree with—even when it seems that they are strong on opinions but weak in the faith department. Remember, they have their own history to deal with. Treat them gently.

For instance, a person who has been around for a while might well be convinced that he can eat anything on the table, while another, with a different background, might assume he should only be a vegetarian and eat accordingly. But since both are guests at Christ's table, wouldn't it be terribly rude if they fell to criticizing what the other ate or didn't eat? God, after all, invited them both to the table. Do you have any business crossing people off the guest list or interfering with God's welcome? If there are corrections to be made or manners to be learned, God can handle that without your help.

Or, say, one person thinks that some days should be set aside as holy and another thinks that each day is pretty much like any other. There are good reasons either way. So, each person is free to follow the convictions of conscience.

—ROMANS 14:1–5 (THE MESSAGE)

Why would God "heal" people from being ADD when He designed them for the benefit of mankind? We need adventurers, warriors, and generals. We need people who will think outside the box and see farther down the road than most. Not everyone needs to be that way, but a certain percentage do.

It was an ADD disciple, Peter, who was willing to jump out of the boat when the rest of them were white-knuckling the sides. Peter, who so many times acted impulsively and spoke without thinking, was the one disciple who willingly jumped out of the boat in order to follow Jesus. He took a risk to walk on water in order to meet Jesus face to face. Forget the potential risk of sinking. In fact, don't even think about it. Jump first, ask questions later. It was Peter the fisherman, the impulsive idea man, the rash one who impetuously cut off an ear in Jesus' defense and was always the first to speak his mind.

It was Peter who raced John to the tomb, and as John hesitated, Peter impulsively burst through. It was Peter, the ADD guy, who was often the spokesman of the other disciples, and upon the "rock" of his confession, Jesus said He would build His church. It was Peter, who died a martyr on behalf of Christ, and others like him, who we so easily consider defective today.

We need people in our lives who act as the rudder, keeping our lives ordered and on course. They offer strength and stability especially in times of rough sailing. Neither the rudder keeper nor the boat jumper is better than the other. Both have a purpose. God created both and all those in between. The lesson we must learn is how to live and work peacefully in the same boat, while enjoying the differences God placed in each of us.

CHAPTER FIVE
Changing Tags

"If a man does not keep pace with his companions, perhaps it is because he hears a different drummer. Let him step to the music which he hears, however measured or faraway."
—HENRY DAVID THOREAU

PHIL'S PARENTS: REV. SYVELLE AND LOVIE PHILLIPS

We always knew that Phil was a special child. When he was only five years old, he was credited with having the vocabulary of a pre-teen. He loved learning, enjoyed reading and having books read to him. He constantly desired to be stimulated and challenged academically. Any parent would be proud to receive the following letter:

Dear Mr. and Mrs. Phillips,

Congratulations. Your son has successfully completed the test for the mentally gifted students in the State of California. Phil's rank is among the top 1 percent of those tested. You are to be congratulated on such an academically gifted student. His school will receive notification of our recommendation to place him in the fifth-grade mentally gifted class.

We were not shocked at Phil's test scores for the mentally gifted. In fact, we were ecstatic. Certainly, this meant a bright future for our eldest son. Our excitement and expectations, however, would be short-lived.

After testing so highly among all the other students in southern California, Phil was placed in the fifth-grade honors class. We did not doubt for a moment that he was smart enough to understand the work and succeed in the class. Not only was the class more academically challenging, it was focused more on written rather than oral skills. As the written workload and the essay-type tests increased, Phil fell behind in his work and began bringing home failing grades.

We received a call from one of his teachers during this time informing us that Phil wasn't applying himself. The teacher believed he was capable of doing the work but just wasn't trying hard enough. We applied more pressure on him to do his best. The problem was, Phil was doing his best, in a nightmare situation for him.

It was during this year when our young son developed a stomach ulcer, no doubt from all the worrying, hand-wringing effort he was putting forth in order to please us, his teachers, and himself. The doctor placed him on a six-week liquid diet. Looking back, it was after the diet ended that Phil began eating out of boredom, frustration, loneliness, and probably sadness.

There was no talk about ADD in the '60s and '70s. We did discover that Phil had a minor form of dyslexia called mirrored vision. This knowledge enabled us to help him read and spell somewhat better. But even with this discovery, the schools either did not or could not make any effort in helping Phil reach

110

his full potential. We all knew the potential was there. We just couldn't figure out why it wasn't being achieved.

It was almost ten years after Phil was married when our daughter-in-law gave us a book on Adult ADD. We found ourselves both devastated and excited in finding there was a name and an explanation for so many of our son's struggles. We had the same thought any loving, concerned parent would have upon finding out in one sitting more than you knew of your child in a lifetime: *If only we had known.* The "if onlys" could have mounted up had we not also been given answers to hard questions.

Caring parents desire above all that their child is happy and healthy in all areas of life. When the child hurts, the parent hurts. When the child succeeds, everyone rejoices. Phil has managed to not only face this misunderstood, misdiagnosed, and complicated issue, but now helps countless others who feel alone and misunderstood.

111

ADD children, regardless of age, need love and affirmation from caring parents. Upon discovering a child is ADD, often we as parents find ourselves in the position of needing to offer an apology to our child for not knowing and understanding the truth sooner. If for no other reason, coming into agreement with him about this revelation of who he is, and why he does the things he does and says the things he says, removes the aloneness that he may have felt throughout his entire life.

Words aren't adequate to express the pride we have in the difficult journey Phil has endured, the gratitude we have in seeing who he really is, and the joy we share with him as he discovers success, joy, peace, and contentment while living out his God-given potential.

When a young boy's father asked the headmaster what profession his son should prepare for, the headmaster curtly replied that it didn't matter. "Your son will never amount to anything."

Years later, this same young man would forget his key, having to awaken his landlady to be let in. Although he could not manage his money or his life, he *could* make sense of the cosmos. The great physicist Albert Einstein would never amount to anything?

Another father of a young boy accused his son of laziness and developed an intense dislike of him that would last a lifetime. He wrote the following letter after his son was accused of cheating on an exam while attending the military academy:

112

> There are two ways of winning in an examination, one credible, the other the reverse. You have unfortunately chosen the latter method and appear to be much pleased with your success. The first extremely discreditable feature of your performance was missing the infantry, for in that failure you demonstrated beyond refutation your slovenly happy-go-lucky harum-scarum style of work for which you have always been distinguished at your different schools.
>
> With all the advantages you had, with all the abilities which you foolishly think yourself to possess and which some of your relations claim for you, with all the efforts that have been made to make your life easy and agreeable, and your work neither oppressive or distasteful, this is the grand result that you come up among the 2nd rate and 3rd rate class who are only good for commissions in a cavalry regiment.
>
> I am certain that if you cannot prevent yourself from leading the idle, useless, unprofitable life you have had

during your schooldays and later months, you will become a mere social wastrel, one of the hundreds of the public school failures, and you will degenerate into a shabby unhappy and futile existence. When that happens, you will have to bear all the blame for such misfortunes yourself.

Sir Winston Churchill would never amount to anything?

It was commonly believed throughout the '80s and well into the '90s that only kids were ADD and that they eventually grew out of it. Many believed that as their nervous system developed and matured, the child's ADD went away, namely the hyperactive component. The medical society now realizes that children do not outgrow ADD; rather, as they mature they learn to adjust to the "disorder" through coping skills and/or medication. And too often, in our experience, many simply learn to muddle their way through life by the school of hard knocks.

One prison warden posed this question: "If ADD is outgrown, why is my prison full of ADD adults?" Studies show that well over 50 percent (some believe as much as 90 percent) of our prison population could have ADD. This is not to imply that the ADD people in our society are immoral people or criminals. However, if you consider the driving, impulsive nature, carelessness in considering consequences, and the need for stimulation (addictive behaviors included), then it is no surprise that many do end up living a life on the opposite side of the law. We do not doubt that factors such as absentee fathers, poor parenting, or an overall bad environment also play a large role in the lives of these people.

It also holds true that over 50 percent of CEOs in Fortune 500 companies are ADD. Again, the difference is usually found by looking at the history of the person, specifically his childhood and the values, principles, and confidence instilled by parents, teachers, and other caregivers.

Some theorists believe that there may be additional types of ADD other than the hyperactive and daydreamer types. One

113

additional form is a child who struggles with control issues, always wanting things done his way. Even still, there are those who would expand well beyond only three types of ADD. There is no doubt that theories will continue to develop and opinions will change on the subject, and as they do, it will remain our goal to offer hope to a large segment of society (children included) who too often are made to feel that they are broken and cannot be fixed.

There undoubtedly is an obvious differentiation between the two most commonly acknowledged types of ADD, the hyperactive type and the daydreamers. Children who are referred to as being ADHD (Attention Deficit Hyperactivity Disorder, or as we like to say, Affectionately Designed Happily Differently!) are the ones whose double dose of energy causes them great difficulty sitting still in school, getting along with other kids, and controlling themselves, as well as problems with aggression and procrastination. Worn-out parents and teachers spend a large majority of their time correcting, corralling, and coercing the more active ADD child in an effort to get the child to behave. These are the children who are prone to accidents—flipping four-wheelers, riding bikes in the street without paying attention, or breaking an arm while performing a new trick on the trampoline.

The daydreamers have many of the same characteristics of ADHD minus the extra energy. They are, as the name implies, dreamers, and often seem "out of it" or stare off into space. They, too, can become easily distracted, struggle in school, and have difficulty paying attention, contending with impulsiveness, or procrastination.

Often, but not always, the ADD and ADHD children will have learning disabilities such as dyslexia that make reading, spelling, and writing even more difficult. Parents have to pay even closer attention to the potential ADD characteristics of the daydreamer child than with the overly active child. Especially at

114

school, the squeaky wheel may get the attention while the quiet, subdued ADD child may not get the assistance he needs.

Children who are ADD exhibit many of the same characteristics as ADD adults. Some may eventually outgrow their hyperactivity, learn to curb their impulsiveness, or develop a system of survival, but ADD will always be a factor in their lives. Again, the biggest difference in the ADD child versus the ADD adult is that the adult knows only too well what is at risk.

Those individuals who discover they are ADD as adults may feel as though they have to make up for lost time. They may need to go back and mend relationships that have been damaged. Others will find themselves looking for a different career that compliments being ADD or change their attitude about their current job. They must often face consequences of past behavior or decisions. They may have graduated from the school of hard knocks, but most ADDers paid a very high tuition.

115

The importance of becoming educated on behalf of the ADD child cannot be overemphasized. An ADD child does not yet understand the consequences of not doing well in school or becoming a social oddity. They cannot comprehend the potential challenges of continued education, future relationships, and a career. They do not yet understand that they *must* learn how to function somewhat as mavericks in a farming world. If not, the consequences can be devastating. The fortunate news is that with parents who are loving and well educated on the subject of ADD, an ADD child has the prospect of a great future while avoiding much of the heartache suffered by so many adults.

One of the most important lessons for children who are ADD is to recognize that, while different from others, they are uniquely designed by God for a special purpose. They must have a clear understanding of who God says they are versus the labels that may have been placed upon them by parents, peers, and other people.

The Color of Your Tag

I once read of a soldier in World War II who was terribly injured on the battlefield. Because of the overwhelming number of wounded, the infirmary had developed a method of identifying who needed the most immediate help by attaching a colored tag to the injured soldiers, unbeknownst to them. A red tag denoted a severe life-threatening injury. Yellow indicated that the soldier had less severe injuries and might survive with medical intervention. The green tag was reserved for those who, if treated immediately, would make it. As the mangled young soldier was brought into the infirmary, he was at once labeled with a red tag.

It is very likely that your ADD spouse, son, or daughter has undergone years of wearing the wrong color of tag.

116

It was said that as the marked man lay dying amid so many other wounded, a nurse was moved to compassion and changed the color of his tag to green. He was consequently moved to the top of the list and received medical attention. Weeks later he would return home having dodged a death sentence placed on him by a tag. He survived a world war and a life-threatening injury because someone changed the color of his tag and gave him a chance.

It is very likely that your ADD spouse, son, or daughter has undergone years of wearing the wrong color of tag. The soldier in the story did not know the color of his tag but rest assured, all ADD people know the color of theirs. No one has kept it from them or even attempted to. No one has offered to change their tags. No one, until now.

Just as the nurse represented life to the young soldier, you represent either life or death to your child. Your words, actions, and attitude toward your child help define who your child is. You, as the parent or the caregiver, represent God to your child. How your child views you is how he will likely view God. How he relates to you is often the way he will relate to God. How he perceives you to feel about him is usually how he will interpret God's view of himself. And it is true that a person's view of himself always determines the direction in which he will gravitate.

Parenting skills make all the difference in the life of the ADD child. This is certainly not to say that good parenting eliminates all the challenges an ADD child faces, but it can and will diminish the negative aspects while allowing the benefits of being ADD to flourish.

While poor parenting does not cause ADD, it can create ADD-like symptoms and certainly exacerbate true ADD symptoms. Often, the "attention deficit" is due to ineffective parental training and involvement. Parenting that is balanced, biblical, and consistent will lay a solid foundation that will last a lifetime—especially for the ADD child who may otherwise suffer needlessly for years.

117

If ADD is viewed as a disorder, then you will attempt to "cure" what is wrong. The ADD child does not have a disease. The ADD child is not broken and does not need to be fixed. There are, of course, those children who are mentally incapable whether due to abuse, a head injury, or a valid disease or sickness. But are we really to believe that millions of otherwise healthy children in this country are incapable of controlling themselves? And that behavioral issues should be modified only by drugs? Should our children who are designed differently believe that a pill can make them smart or help them be kind to others? Are we allowing our children to become mental invalids with little expectation placed on developing internal control and learning life skills?

We would love to know of just one therapist who would first require the parent of an ADD child to obtain solid parental training before writing out a prescription for Ritalin. Our children can control themselves. They do not need a pill to make them smart. They are already smart. They can make friends and control aggression. They can obey and respect authorities, and they can succeed in every aspect of society.

In order for all of us to further understand ADD as a variance, we must ask ourselves some pointed questions: How active must a person be to be considered hyperactive? How impulsive is too impulsive? Is daydreaming a waste of time when creative problem-solving may be taking place? A great hunter counts distractions as one of his greatest assets as a twig breaks or a leaf rustles. Is the distraction a deficit? Many times a talk show guest must be able to use his art of interruption in order to get his view heard. Is this behavior rude or insensitive?

Excess energy, daydreaming, impulsiveness, and interrupting people are all considered negative characteristics of ADD, at least within the society in which we live. Our society is based on order, routine, and schedules. It is interesting, however, to consider if idiosyncrasies in one setting could actually be a positive characteristic in a different environment.

118

While living in Costa Rica, we began to see that the hardships related to being ADD weren't nearly the problem they are when living in the states—especially living in a metropolitan area. Phil had a much easier time feeling "normal" in Costa Rica considering the carefree, docile lifestyle. We often joked that the only time Costa Ricans were in a hurry was behind the wheel of a car! You would almost be considered rude if you showed up on time for a dinner invitation or other event. The unspoken rule of thumb was that everything ran about thirty minutes behind schedule.

A guy on a scooter delivered all our bills to our front door and returned a few days later expecting to be paid in cash. We did not have to bother with writing and recording checks or forgetting about a bill. The entire culture was more relationship-oriented than performance-oriented. It was believed that if you got one major task accomplished a day, it had been a successful day. Days off were taken very seriously and always spent with family or friends. We walked a lot more, ate tons of ridiculously fresh fruits (many of which were picked from our own yard), and enjoyed eating organic beef, free-range chicken, and fish brought directly in from the ocean. We also hired a full-time maid six days a week to cook, clean, and do the laundry —for $150 a month. Pretty ADD friendly, right? Pretty friendly to anyone for that matter!

Now back to reality and our frenetic North American lifestyle. Our family alone has five cell phones, five computers, eight email accounts, a fax machine, three iPods, two websites, and three blog sites. This does not include all the electronic gadgets we have related to our office and ministry. Just about everyone we know lives a fast-paced lifestyle with high expectations, while demanding immediate results and instant gratification. Rare is the family who is able to have a meal together even a few times a week. Once dependent on moral support from grandparents and other family members, relatives now live across the country, leaving too many children to come home from school or spend school holidays at home alone.

By the age of six, the average child will have spent more time sitting in front of the television than he will spend communicating with his father in his entire lifetime. Children influence the $300 billion industry of advertising, including those pesky ADD-friendly thirty-second commercials. Television, video games, and advertising are not only geared for short attention spans but perpetuate any attention problem that may already exist. The remote control was invented for the ADD person— channel surfing typifies their entire makeup!

With the average child spending twenty-eight hours per week watching television, let's consider for a moment what television *cannot* do for a child:

* Television does not help a child develop gross motor and fine motor skills, improve dexterity, or develop spatial or manipulative skills with concrete objects.

119

- Television does not help a child compose sentences, communicate with other people, or develop word games.

- Television does not provide a buddy with whom a child can romp on the floor.

- Television does not help a child explore the full gamut of feelings or learn how to resolve feelings through play. Most programs do little to help a child define his feelings.

- Television does not enhance a child's creativity or his ability to imagine or create positive fantasy.

- Television does not lead a child to ask "What if?" questions. It says to the child, "This is what."

- Television does not provide the variety, the freedom to move, or the problem-solving settings of indoor and outdoor play.

- Television does not provide accurate information by which a child can develop acceptable social behavior. Children need information about people, things, events, relationships, and how society works.

- Television does not provide an accurate portrayal of a relationship with God or a healthy relationship with parents.

- Television does not accurately portray Christians, or give much credence to Christian beliefs or concepts.

- Television does not provide feedback. No other activity in a child's life permits so much intake while demanding so little response.

The question is not whether television, video games, or the like influence children, and in particular the ADD child. The question is, how could they not? The massive surge of ADD diagnoses in the last two decades should come as no surprise with the influx of media to which our children have access. If the ADD child is predisposed to such characteristics as impatience, short attention span, and impetuous behavior, then all these and other characteristics only worsen. The obvious answer to this part of the problem regarding ADD is to control and limit children's consumption of these mediums.

Our overwrought lifestyle, the deluge of media placed upon our children, and the fact that many have simply lost their instinct for parenting, would create an epidemic of ADD-like traits in any society. And in our own society it has caused many children who simply lack stable home lives and effectual parenting to become labeled as being ADD or ADHD, making it difficult to determine genuine ADD from society-induced ADD.

Poor parenting or living in an unhealthy environment does not make a person ADD, at least not in the sense in which we define it. Surroundings and upbringing will affect any child, ADD or not. In our opinion, it is very difficult to know if a child is truly ADD before the age of eight or nine. If effectual parenting begins early in the child's life and is consistently applied, yet both the positive and negative characteristics of ADD prevail, then ADD should be considered. But for the child who has lacked a home environment where standards are set and consequences are established for unacceptable behavior, a diagnosis of ADD or a number of "disorders" can mask problems that stem from inept parenting methods.

121

Medicating the Problem

After attending our parenting seminar, a young mom admitted to us that she had actually coached her nine-year-old son on how to act in the doctor's office in an effort to obtain a prescription for Ritalin. She had experienced so many behavioral issues with her son, and became so frustrated and worn out that she had become willing to resort to medication. Only a couple of weeks later this mom emailed us to say that she had made the effort to put into practice the biblical principles and concepts we had taught, which resulted in a 90 percent decrease in the negative behavior of her son. She said that the child had been on the verge of being kicked out of school and was now making positive progress in all areas—all without medication.

This is not to say that we are against medication in regards to ADD. The right medication can in many cases help the symptoms of ADD, but it will never cure ADD. Yet it is an unequivocal fact that children are too easily medicated in this country and have not been given a fair chance at beating the odds with proper understanding of ADD and functional parenting.

Although children are overdiagnosed as being ADD and subsequently overmedicated, the opposite may be true for adults. We see far too many adults who have no idea why they do the things they do, why they don't do the things they should, or why they have not been able to maintain relationships, keep jobs or, in general, reach their full potential. More often than not, medication can be a lifesaver, or at the very least, an eye-opener.

Our personal rule of thumb regarding medication and ADD is that the ADD individual should first and foremost gain full knowledge about what ADD is and establish a support base (whether in a spouse, family member, or counselor). After a concerted effort is made to understand ADD and find solutions to specific problems, if the ADD individual remains handicapped or paralyzed in a major area of his life, then medication should be considered.

Medication can often give the ADD individual a glimpse of what "normal" is, in the context of our society. The ADDer begins to see some of the reasons why others stay frustrated at them. Medication can help the ADD individual set clear goals and actually accomplish those goals.

After Phil was diagnosed by a doctor as having ADD, he used exercise and natural supplements to help with the procrastination and distraction aspect of ADD. We saw adequate results for a number of years with supplements such as fish oil and Ginkgo Biloba, coupled with early morning exercise. However, as time went on and specifically when Phil had to perform administrative duties, we began to notice that he experienced periods of complete paralysis.

Several years ago I made the journey to my favorite retreat in Colorado in order to finish writing a book. Phil remained at home, left to deal not only with our four children, but also with all the administrative tasks required to run a home and ministry. It was during this time that he had six very important business phone calls to make. He knew it had to be done and so did I. And Phil was the only one who could make the calls.

After three weeks of putting the calls on a to-do list, writing them on a whiteboard, sticking them to a corkboard, and basically torturing himself for being forty years old and unable to make six phone calls, he called me in Colorado completely frustrated and defeated. I reminded him that our family doctor had offered to prescribe him medication if he ever decided to try it.

Phil had become so paralyzed that he had difficulty even making the call to the doctor. He had become completely overwhelmed in every area of his life. And if you are not ADD and don't understand what it is like, you will have no clue what I am talking about. I guarantee you, however, the ADDer will completely relate.

I called the doctor on Phil's behalf and twenty-four hours later he had made all six calls...and paid bills, and straightened his office, and completed a whole new to-do list. The medication gave Phil a serious glimpse of what it was like to be "normal."

Phil remained on medication for a couple of years, after which he got to a place where we felt he might function without it. The medication had helped the fog to lift enabling him to see the path more clearly. I will admit that I liked the results that the medication provided. Phil was much more "farmer-oriented," more organized, neater, and more productive. But the medication also seemed to decrease his creativity and made him, at times, a little cranky.

Medication that is proven to be safe can absolutely help with the negative symptoms of ADD and can prevent much unnecessary heartache and frustration. Medication can also help deal with the potential sidekick problems such as depression—possibly from years of trying to be normal. The point for the ADDer is to be open to what works for him. If a pill helps save his marriage, then it is worth it. If medication is what makes it possible for him to keep a job, then he needs to try it. It benefits him to work with his doctor to find the medication that works for him, keeping in mind that some have side effects. He shouldn't ever hesitate to ask his doctor to adjust the dosage or to change the medicine altogether.

124

Parenting Is the Key

Medication and all its pros and cons aside, the crux of whether an ADD child grows up to be capable of contributing to society, maintaining healthy relationships, and understanding how and why he was created is undoubtedly in the hands of the parent. Everything else is secondary. Parenting is the number one key.

It is not the job of the medical community, the school, or the government to parent our children. It is our responsibility to train, teach, and correct them so they may equate what is taught at home to other venues, such as school and church. It is no wonder that virtually every church in this country has a problem in maintaining teachers for children's ministry, or that some of our best schoolteachers quit the profession. Both are called and desire to teach, but when they have to spend a huge majority of their time trying to get children to pay attention or behave, burnout is common. Teaching cannot take place because training was not applied at home. You cannot teach an untrained child whether at home, school, or church. Teaching deals only with the mind, while training deals with the will.

Many parents fear their own authority in regard to their children, relegating themselves to counselors whose "advice" can simply be ignored. Too many parents view correction as rejection. They fear damaging a child's self-esteem, perhaps because of poor parenting they received as a child. Some resort to pleading or negotiating with their young children to get them to obey. Others just ignore the behavior of their children while becoming oblivious to the future ramifications of doing so. With no consequences for negative behavior, hampered by all the above, the results are tired, frustrated, and hopeless parents.

It is not the job of the medical community, the school, or the government to parent our children. It is our responsibility to train, teach, and correct them.

One ADD "expert," who wrote a book on parenting the ADD child, said that children should be given the attention they need in a positive way when they are behaving well and ignored when they misbehave! This is not only absurd, but also a reflection of our society as a whole in how we so blatantly ignore consequences for poor behavior.

Parents have so easily bought into secular humanism when it comes to training children. In a sense, many parents, even Christian parents, have lost their instinct for parenting and look for a quick fix. They have become so enamored with the world's way that they have become confused and disoriented when their children turn out no better than the kid next door, and sometimes worse. They know there is a better way, but cannot seem to see the truth of the matter. We continue to

125

allow society to dictate to us what is and is not normal, instead of looking to the Word of God and expecting His results by doing things His way.

One of the most important differences between the world's way and God's way of parenting, and other types of instruction for that matter, is that the world will change its mind. What works today will be outdated tomorrow. The Word of God remains the same today, yesterday, and tomorrow. His principles and plan will not require a revised edition. There is a tried and proven way. It is God's way and it is derived from principles taken from His Word and not watered down with meandering secularism.

Rather than basing behavior and social norms on instructions given to us in the Bible, we have depended on psychiatrists, scientists, medical doctors, and even talk show hosts to dictate to us what is "normal." It is not normal to simply ignore belligerence. It is not normal for toddlers or young children to set the tone and standards in the family. It is not normal for our teenagers to go through what has become a rite of passage of anger, rebellion, and destruction. It is not normal for our children to be drugged in order for them to obey. It is not normal for God's people to go through two, three, and four marriages, which are so detrimental to children. Statistics may say it's normal, but statistics lie all the time as to what should be considered normal.

No one can argue that statistics show half of all marriages end in divorce. But while statically true, it is not *normal*. It is easy to look at statistics of current happenings and behaviors in our society in order to substantiate what is, indeed, taking place in our society but again, statistics lie all the time in regards to what is normal, particularly when compared to the standards and principles contained in the Word of God.

The two disciplines that, since their inception, have purposefully set out to remove God from the school, the family,

126

our government, and even our churches have, in our opinion, *caused* many of these so-called mental disorders. Psychology, which originated as a religious study and literally means "study of the soul," has plainly become a science without a soul. Its cousin, psychiatry, meaning "doctoring of the soul," has made every effort to preach a message that is void of biblical values and godly principles. We now find ourselves trying to clean up someone else's mess and repair the damage done over the last several decades. Christian parents, in particular, can no longer turn to a panel of doctors, psychiatrists, or scientists as our authority on spiritual, social, and behavioral norms.

Written by pediatrician Dr. Benjamin Spock in concordance with the psychological agenda of his day, *The Common Sense Book of Baby and Child Care* introduced millions of parents to the Freudian influenced, anti-biblical, free-style form of parenting. First published in 1946, Dr. Spock bought into the concept of passive, permissive parenting, instant gratification, and deviance. Of course, the first generation to grow up on Dr. Spock's erroneous theories were the children of the '60s who celebrated the freedom to have illicit sex, do drugs, burn flags, and, in general, live by the philosophy "If it feels good, do it."

127

Dr. Spock not only became the most famous expert on childrearing, but also amassed great wealth with his book, having sold almost fifty million copies worldwide. Later in his life, however, Dr. Spock publicly announced he had been wrong regarding his theories on childrearing. He offered an apology and came out with a "revised" edition of his book.

This is only one of numerous examples that could be given on those who teach secular humanism as the gospel and then preach it to unsuspecting parents, while changing theories like they would a pair of shoes. The world's way is a gamble, flippant, and opposed to biblical standards. It will always change its mind regarding how our children should be parented. It is like playing a game of Russian roulette with the lives of our children. Sure, some may survive the game, but are the odds really worth taking?

> *For the time will come when they will not endure sound doctrine; but after their own lusts shall they heap to themselves teachers, having itching ears. And they shall turn away their ears from the truth, and shall be turned unto fables.*
>
> —2 TIMOTHY 4:3,4 (KJV)

If left to the world's way, by the time ADD children reach the ages of 10 to 12, some will earn an additional label psychiatrists call "conduct disorder." These are the children who have become more out of control with jet fuel poured on their previously bad behavior. Some are expelled from school, thus beginning what can become a lifelong struggle to function as part of society.

128

Statistics show that 20–40 percent of children who have been diagnosed as having ADHD will develop this conduct disorder, 20–30 percent will experience anxiety disorders, and up to 75 percent will experience depression. The disciplines of psychology and psychiatry often claim that many of these issues stem from ADD, offering an easy excuse for negative behavior.

The Biblical Model

Children are to obey. They are to be kind, patient, and loving. They are to ask for forgiveness when they offend and accept forgiveness from others. They need to learn how to control themselves. They need to respect and respond to their parents and other authority figures. They need to get along with their siblings. This is normal, but it will not happen by osmosis or wishful thinking.

As Christians, we have become alienated from the truth of what is actually normal. We can no longer accept beliefs, values, and principles imposed on us by our culture and society as normal. *We must return to the truth of what is normal*, especially in regard to our children.

During our two decades of dealing with family issues, we have repeatedly seen that the process of blessing can eliminate 80–90 percent of unproductive behavior in older children. This takes place when counterbalanced with the other half of the equation to blessing, which is discipline.

We have become accustomed to hearing the word "discipline" used in a negative manner. Some might describe it as instruction; others interpret discipline to mean that we will right a wrong by means of punishment. While there are as many opinions on what discipline is as there are definitions, for our purposes, we will refer to the definition in Webster's original 1828 dictionary:

> *Discipline: To instruct or educate; to inform the mind; to prepare by instructing in correct principles and habits; as, to discipline youth for a profession, or for future usefulness.*

129

If we use the literal translation of the word "discipline," then as parents we function in the role of *discipler*.

For parents, there is no greater example of a discipler than Jesus. While He was a master teacher to many, He was a loving discipler to a few. He blessed His disciples by knowing them and allowing them to know Him. And because of His unconditional acceptance and love toward them, their hearts were turned toward Him in a radical way. Yet, not only did Jesus walk in the process of blessing the disciples, He also provided the four components of discipline: training, teaching, correction, and reward.

Simon Peter was a fisherman and Jesus *trained* him to be a "fisher of men." Under Jesus' discipleship, a "doubting Thomas" evolved into a missionary apostle and martyr. John went from a "son of thunder," a man known for his temper, to an apostle of love. Jesus took inexperienced, self-directed, and spiritually shallow men and trained them to become mature, capable, and confident ministers of the gospel.

Jesus *taught* values, lessons, and principles to the disciples. He taught them how to pray through His own example, how to love others as themselves, and how to prioritize their lives. He challenged them to forgive the past and prepare for the future.

Jesus, the discipler, brought loving *correction* into the lives of His disciples. In Luke 18:15–17 we find Jesus correcting the disciples for not allowing children to approach Him. In Matthew 26:51–54 Jesus reprimanded brash Peter for cutting off the ear of the high priest's servant in the garden of Gethsemane. Again, in Luke 8:22–25, Jesus rebukes the disciples for their lack of faith during a storm.

Finally, Jesus offered a *reward* to those He discipled. By following Jesus and His instructions, the disciples were rescued from a life of mediocrity: they were given a purpose and destiny, with provision to fulfill their calling. The disciple's greatest reward, however, was a deep, personal and eternal relationship with Jesus Christ.

Our children are our greatest disciples. If we fail to train, teach, correct, and reward them, we have failed in our first and foremost ministry. Scripture instructs us:

> *Train up a children in the way he should go, and when he is old he will not depart from it.*
> —PROVERBS 22:6

The way our children should go is His way—recognizing that God is the ultimate authority in their lives. They learn to respond to His voice by recognizing the authority of, and responding to, the voice of the parents. It is frequently suggested that this proverb actually teaches that one is to train a child "according to his way" (i.e., in accordance with the child's ability, potential, and personality). There is no doubt some truth in this, especially in regard to the ADD child. However, while the expressions may involve consideration for the child's individuality, it is not an accommodation to the child's self-will: the emphasis is still on parental training. This verse plainly states that there is a standard of life to which the child should conform, and it is the parents' responsibility to guide the child in that direction.

Of course, the implication of this Scripture is that there is another way in which children "would" go—their own way. Isaiah reminds us that all of us have a strong tendency to be self-centered and self-directed:

> *All we like sheep have gone astray; we have turned, every one, to his own way; and the LORD has laid on Him the iniquity of us all.*
>
> —ISAIAH 53:6

This is a clear picture of how God defines sin: our becoming self-directed and going our own way. Every child naturally turns to his own way. Children do not need to be taught how to lie, cheat, or disrespect others. If we choose to allow our children to "go their own way," we are abdicating our God-given authority over them.

It is our duty and calling to train our children by establishing firm standards and boundaries for the child. The training goal for young children is obedience to parental control. Until children can control themselves internally, we must provide external control. It is accomplished by setting clear, age-appropriate standards: showing by example and correcting any time the standard is not met. Only when a child is taught values and norms will he develop a strong conscience that is based on more than feelings, urges, and impulses. For the ADD child, this is particularly important. The standards we provide and enforce turn to good habits and eventually become principles that our children will adhere to their entire lives.

One of the most important lessons to be learned by an ADD individual of any age (diagnosed or not, medicated or not) is

131

that *he* is in charge of his behavior and *he* must also own up to the consequences of that behavior. We have now witnessed several generations of children who grew up with little consequences for poor behavior or bad decisions. This is directly related to the moral decline in our society, as well as ineffectual parenting that did not include the four elements in discipline: proper training, teaching, correction, and reward.

Conversely, providing more discipline even as it is defined here, *without* the components involved in the process of blessing (knowing your child, unconditional acceptance, and unconditional love through met needs) will worsen rather than improve the behavior of children with ADD. The ADD child needs everything the average child needs—just more of it. He needs more acceptance, more understanding, more patience, more direction, more supervision, more creative outlets, more correction, more praise.

It also helps to remember that most ADD people, kids included, are not looking for an excuse to keep doing what they are doing. They would change if it were that easy.

132

It is easy to understand how a parent can become frustrated with an ADD child. In particular, the non-ADD parent must guard against assigning judgments against the child who struggles to do things that come naturally to the non-ADD parent or to other siblings. Both parents should look for the ADD child's strengths and help him get better at what he already does well. Much patience and understanding comes from the knowledge gained through a book such as this one. It also helps to remember that most ADD people, kids included, are not looking for an excuse to keep doing what they are doing. They would change if it were that easy. We have never seen an ADDer who would not give anything to not have to struggle so hard to be normal. This is particularly true for the ADD child in the atmosphere of school.

ADD in the Classroom

Parents of ADD children are often perplexed at how challenges with ADD show up so clearly for the child at school, while fewer or none are apparent on weekends or holidays. It does help to understand that our U.S. public school system was modeled after the German school system. The sole purpose of that system was to keep common people out of politics, turn out compliant industry workers, and produce agreeable citizens and soldiers who would not question authority. Creativity and independent thought and action were believed to be problematic in a war, a factory, and in society in general.

During the early years of public education, children attended school only during non-harvest time—around forty-five days per year. Today, not only has the number of days our children go to school been multiplied, but the hours get longer and longer with more homework given than ever before. The majority of our schools remain typically designed to accommodate the farmer-type personality. It requires routine and rote learning which, more often than not, becomes a major source of anxiety, stress, and frustration for the ADD student. It is easy to understand why our most active and creative children in particular have a difficult time in such a restrictive environment, especially if they are easily bored and distracted.

ADD children do have a difficult time sitting still in school and anywhere else where their interest is not piqued. They do not perform as well on standardized tests as other students. They struggle to pay attention and they may well be unorthodox, disruptive, impulsive, or outright antagonistic at times. But this does not mean they are broken, inferior, dumb, or bad. They are different.

When asked about hyperactivity in children, a rabbi in Jerusalem simply replied, "They are more active." He went on to say that, "Hyperactive means too active. Who drew the line?" It is interesting to note that some traditional academies of advanced

Talmudic studies in Jerusalem do not have desks. Each student has his own podium, and the students stand as often as they sit while being taught. It is said that the students can be completely focused from the waist up while dancing like Fred Astaire from the waist down! This serves as a worthy comparison to our own educational system where eight-year-old boys must endure hours of sitting at a desk, day after day.

The average classroom setting is designed for the benefit of the teacher. This is not an effort to denigrate teachers, it is just obvious that it is easier to teach and tolerate students who can sit still, pay attention, take notes, turn in their homework, and raise their hand before speaking. Even standardized tests are convenient ways of measuring the masses, although often providing a false report on whether a student is actually learning versus memorizing.

134

It is important to consider alternative options in education for the ADD child. Our family takes the decision of school on a year-to-year basis, giving thought and prayer to what is best for each of our children, and in particular our ADD son. We are fortunate that the teachers at the school our son attends are very supportive and positive. They genuinely care about him and, although they recognize his challenges in certain areas, they have not allowed ADD to become a crutch or an excuse for not learning.

> *Somewhere between the ages of eleven and fifteen, the average child begins to suffer from an atrophy, the paralysis of curiosity and the suspension of the power to observe. The trouble I should judge to lie with the schools.*
>
> —THOMAS EDISON

Some school districts have the funds necessary to provide special testing and support services for children who are officially diagnosed as being ADD. By law, the ADD child may receive tutoring, extra time or reminders on homework, and other help that encourages learning in a positive atmosphere. It sometimes requires patience and persistence to break into the system, but is worth it for an ADD child who is seriously having difficulty in school or where the parents' options are limited.

Teachers are as much the victim of the system as the ADD child. I have never met a teacher who was in the profession for the money. Teachers want to teach. Yet overcrowded classrooms dictate that teaching is conducted in a method designed for learning styles that are not conducive to most ADD children. In addition, teachers' hands are tied behind their back in enforcing rules and demanding respect and compliance from their students. Even those who know how to command a room full of kids fear being reprimanded (or worse) by administrators or school boards, who, in turn, fear being rebuked by frustrated parents.

Reforming our existing institution of school, re-empowering teachers, and providing stimulating classrooms are all noble goals, but it must begin in the hearts of the parents. It is the parents' responsibility to both bless and discipline their children at home, while instilling a love for learning and a hope for the future.

135

ADD in the Home

In families such as ours where there is an ADD child and an ADD parent, life is rarely boring. In fact, our oldest daughter, Taylor, who is not ADD, wrote the following about her dad:

> I have to admit, having a Dad who announces with no warning, "Hey, kids—pack your bags, we're going on a road trip!" is kind of cool. Most dads would require months of preplanning, budgeting, and preparation, but life with my dad is, well, adventuresome, to say the least.
>
> Of course, the law of gravity dictates that life is not only the ups, but also the inevitable downfalls that ac-

company it. Although sometimes I do long for a "normal" life—you know, where Dad is an accountant, comes home and dutifully announces, "Honey, I'm home." He pats the kid on the head, sits down and watches the evening news—without channel surfing. He has two weeks of planned vacation (put on the calendar one to two years in advance), receives a paycheck every two weeks, has a 401K, and I could go on and on. You know, it's the guy on "Leave It to Beaver." Then again, the Beav and his dad didn't go bungee-jumping, explore the rainforest, travel to Russia, England, Israel—or move to a small country in Central America.

I look at it like this: Anyone can be normal. I'll stick with my abnormal dad, if you don't mind!

Growing up in an ADD home can be fun, adventuresome, hectic, and strange—all wrapped in one. The ADD parent usually possesses the uncanny ability to experience life in a way that makes most normal people cringe. Always ready for a party, the ADD parent is the one to instigate going to fun places, doing crazy things, and living the exciting life. Because the typical ADDer is probably the quickest to forgive when someone wrongs him (and often the quickest to offer an apology), each day is a new day for the ADDer regardless of what may have taken place the day before. This can be a wonderful and almost envious quality of the ADD individual.

The ADDer has days where he feels as though he can accomplish anything, or he has those days where he can be virtually immobile. On the good days, the ADD parent may blissfully proclaim all the wonderful things that are going to be done or bought, or make promises based on the events of that day. He may also make promises out of guilt for his presumed inadequacies. Some ADDers promise things based on the fact that they simply are giving and generous people who have a deep-seated desire to see others happy.

136

The problem with so many promises is when delivery is due, and it falls on a bad day. The children experience disappointment and may develop disrespect or mistrust for the parent. The ADD parent becomes frustrated while creating a never-ending cycle of promises made, promises broken. The non-ADD parent is left to referee between all parties, resulting in feelings of discouragement or anger on her part.

It is wise for the ADD parent to allow the non-ADD parent to buffer any promises with realism, thus helping the ADD parent to guard against making too many unrealistic promises. If this has been a problem, the ADD parent will want to regain the trust of the children by making small, keepable promises.

The importance of involving the entire family about what ADD is, and helping them gain an understanding, cannot be overemphasized. Doing so will drastically hinder the chance of a gap developing between the child and the ADD parent that could have devastating results for a lifetime. Those children who either refuse to understand or who are not presented with the opportunity of knowledge about ADD will often take things personally. Often they respond in hurt, withdrawal, and hesitancy to develop a close relationship with the ADD parent.

137

And not all children respond positively to having an ADD parent. Much depends on the personality and makeup of the child. A child who prefers and functions better with routine or enjoys a clean, ordered house may not appreciate the spontaneity that an ADD parent creates. A serious effort should be made to communicate with all family members on their level about what ADD is and how it can both positively and negatively affect the entire family. Most kids are more than willing to accept that a parent needs a little understanding and help, especially when they see the ADD parent making a real effort. If the children are old enough, ask them to read this book and then ask everyone to make a commitment to maintain open discussions about solutions to problem areas that may arise regarding ADD.

One of the more noticeable characteristics that Phil had with our children was ignoring them. This was not at all intentional on his part. I remember numerous times riding in the car as a family, when one of the children would excitingly want to tell their dad something. "Dad! Dad! Hey, Dad! Guess what? Dad?" Only silence would follow. Again, the dichotomy appears. This man is a great father in so many ways, yet he can come across as insensitive, rude, or uncaring.

Our own children now understand that, at times, they have to get right in front of their dad to ensure getting his attention. More importantly, they have learned not to take their dad's distraction personally. This is why it is very important that everyone who is affected by the ADDer learn to understand the mechanics of how the ADD person acts, responds, works, and lives. Our children know that if their dad is in the middle of trying to complete a project or has just returned from a long trip, it may not be the best time to address complicated matters or even ask for a new pair of basketball shoes. They have learned to wait for a more appropriate time when their dad is not having such a hard time staying focused or trying to be "normal."

Parents must display a unified front with children on all accounts, for if they do not, rest assured that their children will divide and conquer!

138

The ADD adult who may have lived for years not knowing or understanding ADD may begin showing signs of burnout. This happened to Phil in his mid-to late-thirties. He had worked so hard at just being normal that he was facing burnout in every area of his life. He lost much of his desire to succeed, his motivation to keep trying, and had become enshrouded by the ADD fog. Once fun-loving, gentle, and upbeat, the ADD adult may now find himself temperamental or morose, and a little sensitive about negative comments made on his behalf. At one time, the ADDer may have let comments or jokes about his inadequacies slide. Now feeling as though he has nothing to lose, he may find himself lashing out in his own frustration and defeat —no doubt from years of negative labeling and enormous amounts of stress and frustration in trying to be normal.

Because ADD stems from a genetic makeup, it is very frequently passed from one generation to the next. Many adults come to realize that they are ADD only as their own child is diagnosed, recognizing only too well familiar problems that they faced growing up. The ADD parent may respond to the ADD child with complete empathy while remembering his own struggles and childhood pain of trying to be normal. The ADD parent may also react negatively when the ADD child is reprimanded for negative behavior, especially as it relates to ADD tendencies.

Some ADD parents fail to recognize the ADD child's misbehavior, due to distraction, oblivion, or from an out-of-sight, out-of-mind attitude. When the non-ADD parent points out the misbehavior, the ADD parent might explode at the child, feeling guilty for not taking action in the first place. Of course, both the ADD adult and the ADD child tend to forget about infractions quickly. This makes it easy for both to offer and accept apologies but also to dismiss others' hurt feelings.

139

Too often the non-ADD parent feels as though she is raising two children with all the necessary reminders, reprimands, and repercussions. It becomes easy to, in a cry for help, direct anger and frustration toward both the ADD adult and child because they make for easy targets. This is a perfect example of why it is so important to purposefully set aside time for the Devotional Times mentioned in Chapter 3. Parents must display a unified front with children on all accounts, for if they do not, rest assured that their children will divide and conquer!

When a family consists of a parent and child who are both ADD, it becomes critical to avoid negative criticism and labels.

Not only will a child's *you are* statements become for them *I am* statements, but comments made regarding the ADD parent easily transfer to the ADD child, even if the child is not the one being referred to:

> *If Dad is lazy, then I must be lazy.*
> *If Dad is messy, then I am messy.*
> *If Dad is irresponsible, then I must be irresponsible.*
> *If Dad is a failure, then I am a failure.*

Regardless of whether negative comments are intended for the ADD child or not, trust me, ADD kids know they are different. *They know the color of their tag.*

Tragically, neither Albert Einstein nor Churchill knew Jesus as a personal Savior. While both experienced great success in their lives, what really mattered in the end was their eternal destination. Perhaps life would have been different if, as youngsters, both would have grown up with parents and other caregivers who knew them, accepted and loved them, and understood that God wired them for a unique purpose.

Struggles in school, careless accidents, and social inadequacies are all only blips on the screen. The big picture is where the ADD child or any child will spend eternity. One of the first steps toward choosing eternal life with God is understanding who God is, why He so deeply loves and cares for us, and that He calls each of us by name.

Remember in our story of Jacob how God purposefully changed his name to Israel. God recognizes the importance of names and labels. They can heal or kill. Jacob's life was transformed because of the new identity given to him by God. Historically we continue to refer to Israel as Jacob (even Jewish people refer to Abraham, Isaac, and Jacob), showing that labels, even when issued by God, can at times be difficult for others to accept.

But the story of the man who contended with God did not end there.

140

Years later, Jacob's wife, Rachel, would die as the result of giving birth to their son. On her deathbed, Rachel named the boy Ben-Oni, which meant "Son of my pain or sorrow." Jacob then makes one of the most life-giving decisions of his lifetime. Jacob the son, who had effectively lived up to the shoddy name given to him by his mother, became Jacob the Contender, who refused to let go until he experienced the full blessing of God. The one who received a new identity from God now steps in on behalf of his own son and pronounces the boy's name to be Benjamin: "son of my right hand" or "son of good fortune."

> *With her last breath, for she was now dying, she named him Ben-oni (Son-of-My-Pain), but his father named him Ben-jamin (Son-of-Good-Fortune).*
> —GENESIS 35:18 (THE MESSAGE)

Jacob knew far better than anyone else the importance of a name, a tag—a label. And later as Jacob faced his own death, he continued in the process of blessing his son by prophesying a picture of who Benjamin was and of his future (see Genesis 49:27). 141

You have the opportunity to change the tag of the ADD person in your life—a chance to give life, and for many, recall the death sentence placed upon them by society, family, friends, and peers. Make a commitment to begin seeing the ADD person in your life as a great hunter or warrior, a racehorse wired to win. Change your terminology. Paint positive prophetic pictures in your child's life. You can help give him hope for the future, release from the past, and a new beginning that will transform his life—enabling him to fulfill his greatest potential.

CHAPTER SIX

What Are You Going to Do With Your Wild Ass?

"If you act like an ass, don't get insulted if people ride you."
—YIDDISH PROVERB

PHIL PHILLIPS

I would like to take this chapter to address the ADD person. If you think there is even a remote possibility that you might be ADD, if you read nothing else, read this part. Yes, it would help you to read the book in its entirety (or at least listen to the audio version), but if you aren't ready to do that it's okay. But for now, there are some things you should hear directly from an ADDer.

One of my most outstanding "ADD moments" that I can remember as a child happened when my parents were traveling evangelists. I was a scruffy preschooler when my dad sold everything we had in order to purchase a thirty-foot Airstream travel trailer in which we wound up living for three years. (These trailers are considered cool today, but back then it reminded me of an aluminum turtle going down the road!)

During one of our travels, we pulled off at a rest stop in the New Mexico/Arizona desert. It wasn't a nice, neat rest stop like we have today—only a dusty wide spot in the road. Enjoying the break, I got out and started running around with my dog. My dad had spotted a large hole, brought it to my attention, and told me not to go near the hole—which only poured jet fuel on my ADD curiosity, thus giving way for the ADD impulsiveness to take rein.

In an effort to "show off" for my dad, I placed him next to the white Chrysler and aluminum turtle so he could see my every move. For a split second, Dad turned his back and I headed for the forbidden hole. Before either of us knew it, I had fallen in.

This hole was not your average, ordinary hole. It was about five feet deep and five feet wide. However, the depth and width were not what made this hole special. This was a very special hole for, you see, it was where the trailers dumped their sewage. And the hole happened to be full that day, and I wasn't born six-foot, four-inches tall!

I bobbed up and down in the hole before my father could reluctantly put his hand in and pull me out. I spent the next three hours in a compromising position in order to get cleaned up enough to get back in the car with my parents. And no matter how gross you just envisioned that scenario to be, believe me, it was worse, much worse.

This is where I see so many Christians today: trying to do their own thing and ending up doing something stupid. Or we burn ourselves out trying to give God what He never really asked for in the first place. This is particularly true for the ADDer who has to work overtime just to do the right thing, say the right thing, keep the right job, stay focused, don't interrupt, and keep up with the myriad of duties in life. We are often drawn to the forbidden hole because we lack understanding of our need for stimulation, risk-taking, adventure, and change.

Finding out I was ADD was one of the greatest things that ever happened to me. It also was one of the most upsetting. I was excited that there was finally a very real answer to my unorthodox, nonconformist, almost heretical-type ways. I was also glad to put a finger on why everyone seemed to stay perturbed at me, and why I was always the easy target. It made a lot of sense and made a very real difference in how I saw myself. It also helped to realize that others were standing on some pretty solid ground as to why they felt the way they did toward me.

Throughout this book, it is made clear that we don't believe that ADD is a disorder. You are not sick, broken, or stupid. You will never be cured of ADD because God wired you the way He needed you to be. The sooner you can grasp that concept, the quicker you can get on down the road and deal with being designed differently.

Finding out I was ADD was one of the greatest things that ever happened to me...It made a lot of sense and made a very real difference in how I saw myself.

145

It will be of little benefit to dwell on the wake of destruction that may have been left behind during your pre-knowledge days of being ADD. Yes, you may need to go back and mend some fences, but rather than focusing on problems, you have got to start looking for what works for you and then do it! No longer should you settle for trying to peer through the fog. The fog can and will lift as you now enter the ADD world with a clearer view and from a position of strength rather than weakness.

Someone once said that we either make ourselves miserable or we make ourselves strong, and the work is about the same. Which are you right now: miserable or strong? Are you wallowing in past failures, broken relationships, and ruined career, or crying over the fact that you didn't know you were ADD until now? Or are you passionate about life, motivated to do the right thing for the right reasons, while understanding that life is not a dress rehearsal? You have only one shot to reach your full potential while on this earth.

Please don't think that knowing you are ADD is what creates your position of strength. While it certainly is a big key, what really is the foundation for this position is understanding that you are, pardon the expression, "a wild ass." Now, before you throw this book in the recycle bin, understand that I didn't call you a wild ass; God did.

An Untamed Nature

Like a good baseball umpire, God usually calls things the way He sees them, and He describes us as wild-ass men. The wild ass, or untamed donkey, while known for its strength, is prone to stubbornness and perverseness. God frequently painted these graphic, emotive pictures that expose our obstinacy and desire to be self-directed and self-sufficient. ADDers love this kind of verbal bluntness. It gives a spark to ignite their fire, to light their pathway through the fog. Too often we have allowed our Christianity to become so feminized that we forget that God at times uses frank, manly-man terms to deal with us.

The donkey is mentioned frequently throughout the Bible, which is not surprising since it was one of the most useful animals in Bible times. Caravans of donkeys would compare to our modern-day convoy of transport trucks. Although the donkey was one of the first animals in the Bible to be tamed, God compares our sinful nature to that of an untamed donkey or wild ass, providing us with an allegory of things to come. It paints a picture in big broad strokes of what Jesus would do for us.

> *A wild ass, used to the wilderness, that snuffeth up the wind at her pleasure; in her occasion who can turn her away? All they that seek her will not weary themselves; in her month they shall find her.*
>
> —JEREMIAH 2:24 (KJV)

It's interesting to note that when a donkey is mentioned in the Bible, it is usually in conjunction with a man who is doing something destructive or, at very least, going his own way. This is not true in the representation of other animals such as the lion, eagle, or dove. The wild ass represented a cantankerous, self-directed, hard-to-control animal. Sound like anyone you know?

Well, if it doesn't ring a bell, there were those recorded in the Bible who were referred to as wild-ass men. Issachar, one of the sons of Jacob and Leah, was one of them. As Jacob blessed him, he described Issachar as a "strong ass couching down between two burdens" (Genesis 49:14, KJV). Hmm…is that a compliment? Actually, it was quite flattering. The strong-boned donkey had a great capacity for carrying heavy burdens and would signify Issachar's strength and endurance, particularly on the battlefield.

Ishmael, the son of Abraham and Hagar (Sarah's Egyptian maid) was another wild-ass man. God spoke the following of Ishmael:

147

He shall be a wild ass of a man, his hand against every man and every man's hand against him; and he shall dwell over against all his kinsmen.
—Genesis 16:12 (RSV)

The Message translation reads this way:

From this pregnancy, you'll get a son: Name him Ishmael; for God heard you, God answered you. He'll be a bucking bronco of a man, a real fighter, fighting and being fought, Always stirring up trouble, always at odds with his family.
—Genesis 16:11,12

If you think your family unit was strange, you should consider the family Ishmael was born into. Although sired by Abraham, Ishmael's life went haywire when Sarah got pregnant with Isaac, the son who would be his father's true heir.

Ishmael, already tagged by God as having a wild streak about him, had the flames fanned by a mother who did what scorned women do best: planted seeds of hatred, anger, and fear in her son. By the time Ishmael entered his teenage years, he no doubt reflected his mother's disregard for Sarah and her son. During a celebratory feast, Sarah's maternal instinct snapped when she saw Ishmael mocking Isaac, and ordered Hagar and her son to get out of town.

It is easy to think of Ishmael as being the cursed son, although this is not at all true. Ishmael was wired to be strong, fierce, and free-spirited. God made it very clear that, not only did He care about both Hagar and Ishmael, but He would protect Ishmael and provide him with a blessing as well.

One of the relationships I find most fascinating takes place in Genesis 21:14–20:

148

> *So Abraham rose early in the morning, and took bread and a skin of water; and putting it on her shoulder, he gave it and the boy to Hagar, and sent her away. Then she departed and wandered in the Wilderness of Beersheba.*
>
> *And the water in the skin was used up, and she placed the boy under one of the shrubs.*
>
> *Then she went and sat down across from him at a distance of about a bowshot; for she said to herself, "Let me not see the death of the boy." So she sat opposite of him, and lifted her voice and wept.*
>
> And God heard the voice of the lad. *Then the angel of God called to Hagar out of heaven, and said to her, "What ails you, Hagar? Fear not, for God has heard the voice of the lad where he is.* (emphasis added)

After being run out of town, Hagar, an Egyptian slave and a single mom, finds herself lost in the desert with her son and with no provisions. She becomes distraught over the fact that death is inevitable. Not wanting to witness her own son's death, she leaves him under what little shade the bushes would afford. In her anguish, she cries a mother's cry and God responds with a Father's heart.

Although the angel spoke directly to Hagar, it was the plea of the wild-ass boy that gained God's attention. His cries brought heavenly intervention. Ishmael, the wild one, the descendant of Abraham whose name meant "God hears," had access to the ear of God. Both Isaac and Ishmael, one a faith-based child and the other a flesh-based child, had value to God.

Notice something else: God has heard the voice of the lad *where he is.* You mean Ishmael didn't have to change or prove he could control his wild nature? That God would meet him right where he was—broken, hurt, angry, thirsty, and dying? That God would take a wild man whose lineage remains the root of alienation between Christians and Muslims today, and *hear his voice?* Absolutely!

Through adversity, God was trying to bring Ishmael into submission, proving that while God hears, He does not always approve. And though He may not approve, for those who desire to receive His gift of adoption, He accepts even the most untamed ass.

The passage continues to give us great revelation as to God's presence and provision in our lives:

> *"Arise, lift up the lad and hold him with your hand, for I will make him a great nation."*
> Then God opened her eyes, *and she saw a well of water. And she went and filled the skin with water, and gave the lad a drink.*
> *So* God was with the lad; *and he grew and dwelt in the wilderness, and became an archer.*
> —GENESIS 21:18–20 (EMPHASIS ADDED)

Through her anguish and tears, Hagar could not see that the solution to her problem was right in front of her! It took God giving her an accurate viewpoint, a clearer vision, in order for her to gain access to the water that would give life. Present-day Muslims, during pilgrimages to Mecca, reenact the frantic search by Hagar to find water as they run between the hills of Safa and Marwa. The search concludes as they reach the sacred well of ZamZam where they not only sip the water as a reminder of God's mercy to Hagar, but also believe the water to be holy, containing healing properties.

Islam denies Muslims the knowledge and saving grace of the true Living Water who Christians know to be Jesus. It is a non-negotiable, historically proven fact that only Jesus can quench our thirst—not Muhammad, a physical well, a better job, more money, a great spouse, or a pilgrimage around the world. It is only Jesus who can satisfy the deepest longing to live—*really* live.

Ishmael was blessed with twelve sons, and some believe that he did eventually embrace the faith of his father, Abraham—confirming that seeds planted in the lives of children will one day come to fruition. Ishmael would continue in many respects as a wild man, living in the wilderness and becoming an expert archer. The restrictions of city life with all its advantages and conveniences were not for him. And just as boot camp makes a good soldier, surviving the desert made a man of Ishmael.

Although God would remain with Ishmael throughout his life, his lineage would produce wild and untamed hearts in the name of Mohammed. Little did Sarah know when she persuaded Abraham to have a child by Hagar, that she was instigating an enmity which has continued with severe intensity through the ages.

Submitting to God's Will

God is sovereign and rules with both mercy and justice; yet, if we gravitate toward our untamed nature, we are going to wind up in a place of dryness or loneliness. The wild-ass person who does not submit to God's will in his life will eventually end up wandering alone in the desert, without direction. Their thirst will never be quenched by self-direction and self-sufficiency.

They sow the wind, and reap the whirlwind. The stalk has no bud; it shall never produce meal. If it should produce, aliens would swallow it up. Israel is swallowed up; now they are among the Gentiles like a vessel in which is no pleasure. For they have gone up to Assyria, like a wild donkey alone by itself...

—HOSEA 8:7–9

God, in His scornful rebuke to Job, refers to the wild, untamed donkey:

"Who set the wild donkey free? Who loosed the bonds of the onager, whose home I have made the wilderness, and the barren land his dwelling?"

—JOB 39:5,6

In each of our lives, God attempts to bring us to a place of submission. God doesn't want to break our spirits, especially those of us He created to have a wild, passionate side. He can use adventuresome, creative, and strong individuals—as long as we bridle our will to His and allow our wild side to be influenced and tempered by Him. And when we do allow God to work through us, some peculiar and incredible things can happen. Consider the story of Balaam and his donkey—one of the more famous Bible stories found in Numbers chapter 22.

Balaam is something of a prophet-for-hire guy. I imagine him as a wheeler-dealer type who wore gold chains, a pinky ring, and cheap cologne. He tries at times to do the right thing but is too often sidetracked by his lust for gain.

Balak, the Moabite king, decides that the Israelites needed to have a curse placed upon them, as they were too strong of a foe. He sends messengers to Balaam (who must have had a pretty good reputation for his accuracy in cursing and blessing), and they try to hire him to do the deed. Always the accommodating host, Balaam asked them to spend the night so that he could confer with God about the job. During the night, God reminded

151

Balaam that the Israelites were a blessed people and that he was not to curse them.

When the messengers returned home without Balaam, the king then sent higher-ranking emissaries who sweetened the pot by offering more money and an exalted position. Again, Balaam seeks God another night for "clarification." At this point, Balaam, although speaking the right words, decides to become self-directed.

He saddles up his donkey and begins the journey toward reversionism (going backward in one's spiritual life). When prophets, pastors, and other spiritual leaders enter into spiritual digression, they are twice as destructive, as we shall see in our story.

> The man who doesn't let God rule him is lowered beneath the donkey who does.
>
> —UNKNOWN

On the way to Moab, an angel holding a drawn sword appeared in the pathway. The prophet didn't see the angel, but the donkey sure did. In an attempt to avoid the angel, the donkey veered off the path into a field. Balaam lashed out at the donkey, and as he tried to continue on the path, the angel of the Lord was standing in a narrow area between two walls, forcing the donkey to crush Balaam's foot against the wall. Balaam, in his state of spiritual blindness, could not see the angel and began whipping the donkey. The angel of the Lord then moved around until he stood in a place so narrow that there was no room to pass on the right or left. The donkey took evasive action by collapsing under Balaam, enraging him to the point of beating the donkey even harder.

Balaam was already having a bad day, and to add insult to injury, God opened the mouth of the donkey and she began asking him some pointed questions: "Why are you beating me when I've always been a pretty good donkey to you?" I am not sure which is stranger here—the fact that the donkey actually spoke, or the fact that Balaam responded to the speaking donkey as though it were a common occurrence. There was a reason the donkey behaved the way it did, but Balaam was being too stubborn to recognize that God was trying to get his attention. God was trying to intervene on behalf of a blessed people and was willing to use a donkey if necessary.

The donkey is often represented as being a self-directed stubborn animal when often it is using its skill for self-preservation. Though donkeys are sure-footed, they can be easily distracted. The donkey doesn't fight back when beaten down. They have a short memory and attention span. They forgive easily. Balaam, rather than give the donkey credit for years of faithful service, instead chose, in his self-righteous arrogance and in an attempt to relieve his own guilt, to beat the donkey into submission—making him the chief ass in this remarkable story.

The beleaguered donkey became an instrument used by God as part of the divine plan. The donkey was exceptional and special not because she asked to be, but because she was chosen to be that way. Yet, the donkey that saved Balaam's life was only rewarded with additional verbal and physical abuse by him—never fighting back, rebelling, kicking, or losing control.

153

The world is full of Balaams who are shortsighted, ignorant, and walk through life with their eyes shut—oblivious to God's presence in their lives and His desire to protect each of us from going our own way and doing something stupid. Balaam was willing to entertain the thought of cursing God's chosen people because of his blinded stupor and lustful greed. It was only after a direct confrontation with God that Balaam awoke from his spiritual blindness. And although he did not carry through with his intent to pronounce the curse, his entertaining and aiding the enemies of Israel would later cause the death of 24,000 Israelites.

Galatians 1:4 tells us that Jesus gave Himself for our sins to free us from this evil world we live in. The sacrifice that Jesus made stands between you and your past, between you and your environment, and between you and your self-direction.

We are given an allegory (that happens to involve a donkey!) in the Old Testament of this sacrifice that took place on our behalf:

> *But every firstborn of a donkey you shall redeem with a lamb; and if you will not redeem it, then you shall break its neck. And all the firstborn of man among your sons you shall redeem.*
> —Exodus 13:13

In order to save the donkey, something had to be sacrificed and blood had to be shed. The only way that the donkey could escape getting its neck broken was if a lamb was offered in its place. The donkey had little value until exchanged for the lamb. Because of its wild nature, the donkey deserved to have its neck broken. Yet God valued even the donkey enough to provide a method of deliverance from a death sentence.

God offers this same way out for us today. Though we were self-directed, wild-ass men, He became the sacrificial lamb on our behalf. He did not ask that we bury our individuality, only that we submit our will to His. While here on earth, Jesus could have used His divine attributes independently from the Father, yet He denied His divine self. The same temptation exists for the unbridled man who attempts to use his abilities and giftings in order to create independence. If you spell the word "flesh" backwards and drop the "h," you get the word "self." Flesh is self and self is flesh as long as your wild-ass nature dominates who you are.

The alternative is to "walk in the Spirit" (Galatians 5:16), "be led by the Spirit" (Galatians 5:18), and "live in the Spirit" (Galatians 5:25).

When God created man as an intelligent being, He gave us a choice to be self-directed. Hell originated as a place of pun-

154

ishment for Satan, who embraced himself to the exclusion of God. He fell, and all that followed his direction fell with him. The enemy continues to whisper to the untamed man, "Be god. Be independent. Make your own way. Do your own thing. Determine your own future."

The Lord of glory took on the flesh of the wild-ass man. When Jesus becomes the controlling factor in our lives and we respond to the sacrifice that was placed on the mercy seat, we gain dignity that comes *only* through Him.

> For the life of the flesh is in the blood, and I have given it to you upon the altar to make atonement for your souls; for it is the blood that makes atonement for the soul.
> —LEVITICUS 17:11

Because our very nature is one of self-direction and self-sufficiency, God confronts it directly. He knows that we will create a god of our liking, a god that symbolizes part of our nature, a god in our own image. We will create a god that values the donkey more than the Creator, enabling the donkey to do its own thing.

Some years ago when Cynthia and I were the family pastors at a large church in the Dallas area, we were commissioned by the senior pastor to create and present an illustrated sermon for Palm Sunday. It goes without saying that if you are serious about making Palm Sunday really special, you need a donkey. The request to do this special sermon came only two weeks before Palm Sunday so I found myself frantically searching for a donkey to rent. I not only found a donkey, but also got it for a great price—or so I thought. (There is something to the old adage of getting what you pay for!)

Our church had just completed a brand-new sanctuary, probably one of the most beautiful structures in the country. Designed in a Texas cathedral style, it was stunning in every regard—in particular the very expensive fleur de lis carpet that had been shipped in from England.

On the morning of Palm Sunday, the donkey and his owner arrived at the church in time to do a practice run. All seemed well. The owner/trainer assured me that the donkey was trained to "do his business" before the performance so no mishaps would occur. No problem, right? Wrong! Big time wrong. As "Jesus" came riding down the center aisle surrounded by thousands of palm-leaf-waving congregants—the lowly little donkey did a doo on the imported carpet! Jesus' triumphant entry became a stinky situation in which the donkey and I both lost our dignity. (And no matter how bad you just envisioned this scenario to be, it was worse. Much worse.)

When the real Jesus rode into Jerusalem on the back of a donkey, it is important to understand that what gave the animal dignity was the one who held the reins. Jesus was in control and the donkey served the purpose God had intended of symbolizing the eternal message of forgiveness and peace.

Yet in the world in which we live, more value is placed on the donkey than on what God is able to do through the donkey. In essence, this is the practice we now know as humanism where values, characteristics, potential, and behavior are believed to be accredited to human beings, rather than to any supernatural authority.

The value of the donkey is directly related to the image of God. When we are subjected to and directed by God, we give the Holy Spirit control of the reins, bridling our will to His.

Even though we are new creatures and our spirit man is completely altered, we still are in a battle with our flesh. We need to be conformed to the image of Christ on a daily basis if we are to defeat the duality of our nature. Our hope is found in Jesus who became the substitute for our wild, untamed nature. And the empowerment that comes from the Holy Spirit enables even the most wild at heart creature to live a tamed life.

156

Again, the Word says in Isaiah 53:6 that we have *all* gone astray, ADD or not. Of course, being an ADDer, we seem to see more clearly the fact that we have fallen short of the mark. And if we don't see it for ourselves there are enough people out there to remind us of it. The labels placed upon us seem to have moved us to the top of the "falling short" list. Yet, we *all* deserve to have our necks broken.

> *We're all like sheep who've wandered off and gotten lost.*
> *We've all done our own thing, gone our own way.*
> —ISAIAH 53:6 (THE MESSAGE)

There is a spiritual fog that can engulf a person, often keeping him from seeing God for who He really is—a perfect Father. There is nothing you can do to make God love you any more. You didn't make Him love you in the first place. It wasn't as though you "courted" His love, acceptance, or favor. He freely gave it to you the moment you placed your trust in Christ. He took a thousand steps, maybe more, toward you before you even thought about approaching Him.

Not only does the fogginess keep us from seeing who God is, it also blurs who we are in Him. It may have been years since you have dealt honestly with yourself about who you really are (or maybe you never have). Being ADD, you have probably worn the faulty pair of glasses we referred to earlier. You may not even know where to draw the line between truth and lies. You were told you were lazy, now you believe it to be true. It must be true. You are irresponsible; you just can't get the job done. If only you would think before you act. You are insensitive. You are selfish. Blah, blah, blah. You have gone long enough without challenging the labels put on you.

If someone were to accuse you of being a baby killer, you would consider that ridiculous. You've never harmed a child. Factually you know better. You are a kind, law-abiding, decent

157

person. As a result, this label doesn't become a factor in your life. You naturally shut the door on it.

The problem lies among the more objective labels. You need to put to the test the labels and perceptions that others have placed on you (or that you have placed on yourself). Are you a liar? Probably not. You have good intentions, but may have a difficult time following through with things. Are you stupid? Very, very doubtful. Most ADDers have a very high IQ —we just have a harder time demonstrating how smart we really are. Are you lazy, or do you work differently from others? Are you insensitive? No, you just don't always think before you speak.

As an ADDer, you have natural gifts that have been given to you. Find out what these are and then use them to benefit every area of your life.

158

As an ADDer, you have natural gifts that have been given to you. Find out what these are and then use them to benefit every area of your life. For instance, ADDers are usually quick to forgive—every day is a new day. This can be a great asset to have in any relationship. We are usually positive thinkers who see the glass as half full versus half empty. Another great quality. If you have experienced burnout from not knowing you were ADD, then you may have to rediscover some of these qualities—but they are there, even if buried beneath years of untruth.

We all must allow God to classify who we are. When we give others permission to define us then we also give them permission to mold us in their image. We need to begin acting like adopted sons or daughters of the Living God. And just as if your body were exposed to nuclear material, you cannot help but be changed! You are not going to act like Jesus; you are going to be like Jesus. You will not ask what would Jesus do. Rather, you will live in Jesus Christ and He will live through you. Start acting like you are smart. You are responsible because He is responsible. You are fun-loving. You are creative. You are who God made you to be.

Several years back in an effort to give my physical body a little tune-up, I decided to go have a coffee colonic. Yep, it's where they place you on a table, insert…well, forget the details. Anyhow, as I was lying on the table, I noticed the strategically placed sign on the ceiling that read:

Let go and let God.

There were so many preacher illustrations that flooded my mind at that moment, one of which was to consider that when we do let go and let God, the you-know-what comes out. (And at this point, I am now wondering to myself how the last chapter of such a great book could go to pot.)

God is the only one capable of taking our messed up lives shrouded by a stubborn, obstinate will and cleaning us up. It's what He does and who He is. Too often we view God's fatherly correction as rejection, yet we should feel as David did—comforted when God proves through His correction that we are not illegitimate children.

God's correction in our lives is His effort to make us more like Him. It creates maturity and Christlikeness. It reminds us to remove our hands from our own lives and allow Him to do away with those things that do not conform to the image of Christ.

The Italian artist and sculptor Michelangelo is best known for his marble statue of David. His second most famous work is the fresco on the ceiling of the Sistine Chapel. Michelangelo (who was probably ADD himself, working for over forty years on a project commissioned by the Pope and never completing it) would first envision in his mind the end-product of his project.

Before Michelangelo began the carving of David out of the eighteen-foot-high block of marble, he first envisioned the end

159

result. (God knows what He has in mind for you and already envisions the completed outcome.) It was said that the artist then began chipping away from the stone anything that did not line up with his mental picture. (This is how God works in us: He whittles away those things that do not line up with His plan for our lives. He gets rid of idols, faulty plans, unruly wills, and anything else that stands between us and Him.) When the artist was asked how he had created a masterpiece from a mere block of marble, he purportedly answered that he simply chipped away everything that didn't look like David.

As we allow the Master Sculptor to mold us and cut away anything in our lives that is not a reflection of His image, a work of art emerges in each of us. God can remove the broken pieces of anger, hurt, and pain that may have been caused from years of just not knowing. He chisels our bitterness and unforgiveness into smoother, more manageable forms. He allows dreams that have been trapped in stone to emerge. He makes us more compassionate, more creative, more useful, and more like Him.

160

An Action Plan

I know this chapter (not to mention the entire book) may be hard to digest for the newly discovered ADDer. There probably hasn't been a lot of opportunity in your world for focusing on your spiritual life when you are in survival mode. It has probably been very difficult just trying to be normal and keeping everyone at peace with you. But the one thing you must understand is that *we are in a battle.* A fierce battle. Your purpose on this earth is directly related to the purposes of God. And God needs you to be healthy and strong. You are a frontline warrior who must know when to charge and when to retreat. And believe me, it is much easier to withdraw than it is to remain in the fight, staying focused, and determined to fulfill your destiny.

God's gifts and God's call are under full warranty—never canceled, never rescinded.
—ROMANS 11:29 (THE MESSAGE)

I understand as a fellow ADDer that, at times, it is our own hesitation that holds us back from doing what God gifted us to do. We have the ability, yet we have become gun-shy, too often because of being shot over and over again by friendly fire. The labels placed on us have become our realities; true or not, they have become our perspectives. When labels are coupled with failures and accusations of character flaws, a hesitancy is created in your spirit that blocks you from trying again.

> *What lies behind us and what lies before us are tiny matters compared to what lies within us.*
> —RALPH WALDO EMERSON

I was labeled all my life as being uncoordinated. It stuck with me until one day, in my thirties, my friend and personal trainer in self-defense, looked at me and asked, "Who lied to you?"

He said that someone, somewhere told me I was uncoordinated. He called the lie out of hiding and brought it to light.

He went on to say that I had the athletic ability of a college athlete—no more, no less. He explained that, although I learn differently, I was in no way uncoordinated. I then began seeing myself as that college athlete—coordinated and capable.

> *Sometimes it is not good enough to do your best; you have to do what's required.*
> —SIR WINSTON CHURCHILL

Regardless of how difficult it is when you feel you have done your absolute best and can do no more, there are some things that are *required*. The following are a few examples and should never be considered optional or up for negotiation:

161

- Faithfulness and loyalty to your spouse.

- Honesty and integrity in every relationship from your spouse to your creditors.

- Creating and maintaining security for your family—keeping in place those things that are important such as a job, savings accounts, health insurance, and life insurance.

- Refusing to make decisions that are detrimental to yourself or your family (e.g., quitting a job before another one is in place, or without agreement from your spouse). If you do blow it in any area, own up to the behavior and accept the consequences.

- Never use ADD as a crutch or excuse for poor behavior, or for those things you just don't want to do. Being ADD is an explanation not an excuse. If you are constantly referring to ADD as the reason for everything that goes wrong in your life, you will weaken others' efforts to trust you when it really is an ADD issue. In other words, you can't afford to cry wolf too often.

162

What you can afford to do is enlist some trusted individuals to be on your team. Give them permission to hold you accountable in all areas or to help get your attention when the wild-ass nature wants to resurface.

Some qualified people might include:

- Your spouse

- A close friend

- A trusted coworker

- Your pastor or other spiritual leader

- Your mom or dad

- Your adult child

✦ A professional counselor or life coach

Brothers, choose seven men from among you who are known to be full of the spirit and wisdom.
—ACTS 6:3 (NIV)

A comedian once said that if your ship doesn't come in, swim out to it. That is exactly what you need to do beginning today. It is your choice to clear the slate and endorse a plan of action. In fact, it just so happens that I am going to get you started with this action plan. Study the following acronym for that very word, A-C-T-I-O-N. You need to post it on your computer, mirror, or dashboard, and commit it to memory. Do whatever it takes to get it in your head and heart.

A — ACKNOWLEDGE

163

Your first step toward turning your world right-side up is simply to acknowledge that you are not stupid, lazy, or worthless. Your Creator purposefully wired you in a unique way. You are not defective, not a loser, and can live up to your full potential. You are Affectionately Designed Differently!

C — CHOOSE

An old Alcoholics Anonymous saying states that change occurs when the pain of remaining the same is greater than the pain of changing. Many who have unknowingly lived with being ADD need change. They have experienced great disappointment, frustration, brokenness, and embarrassment. The choice is yours whether to live in denial of being wired differently, or to accept the fact that you are an intelligent, hardworking, caring, and unique individual. God made you in a different kind of way, for a different kind of purpose, and it is now time to choose to accept your uniqueness. This choice may involve a time of grieving over past losses such as failed relationships, missed career opportunities, or a wake of hurt, disappointment, and loss in other areas of your life.

Regardless of the type of loss you incurred, grieving is often needed and is perfectly acceptable. You may want to cry alone or with someone who deeply cares about you. You may need to have a "discussion" with God. But you and you alone must choose to forgive everyone involved: yourself, your parents (perhaps for not knowing that you were ADD), teachers, well-meaning friends, pastors, and, yes, even God. (No, God does not benefit from you offering forgiveness. *You* are the one who reaps the benefit!)

T — TREATMENT

Before you assume that I am referring only to medication or counseling, realize that I am first talking about getting seriously educated about ADD. If you were unable to read this book in its entirety, get the audio version. *Do what it takes to become educated.*

164

You may need to get an official diagnosis of being ADD for two reasons. First, more often than not, there are underlying issues that accompany ADD, especially in adults who are only now finding out they are ADD. These can include depression, anxiety, or damaging addictions. These and possible other "sidekicks" should be diagnosed and treated by a trusted physician. Second, the symptoms of being ADD may need to be treated with medication. You may reason that if being ADD is not a disorder, rather a unique wiring by God, why then would one take medication?

This is a fair question but one that must be considered in relation to the society in which we live. In other words, we don't necessarily live in an ADD-friendly world. Some aspects do make it easier for the ADD individual to survive, such as cell phones, PDAs, beepers, and fast food! Yet our typical work schedule, others' expectations, and pressure to live routine, organized, normal lives are very real factors with which you have to deal.

Attempting to live like a non-ADDer can wear you out, beat you up, and leave you feeling overwhelmed, frustrated, and hopeless. It doesn't have to be that way.

As was previously mentioned, our personal rule of thumb regarding ADD and medication is this: When a person becomes handicapped or paralyzed in a *major* area of life—whether in a marriage relationship, job, or school—because of characteristics associated with being ADD, then medication should be considered. And again, if there are coexisting problems such as depression or anxiety, then medication can be a lifesaver.

Some ADDers try medication in order to experience what being "normal" feels like. After they get a clearer view of what they need to be doing, they find some skills or alternative ways of dealing with ADD to help them accomplish their goals.

Counseling or life coaching can also be a tremendous benefit to the newly discovered ADDer. No doubt years of pain and resentfulness may be present with many who discover as adults an explanation to so many unanswered questions. More often than not, marriage relationships, parent-child relationships, and even work relationships have suffered because of the ramifications of not knowing and understanding the components of ADD.

We cannot discount receiving treatment from our ultimate Counselor. His perspective on who you are is critical to your healing and future progress. God made you in a fearful and wonderful way. He knows you, and He understands, accepts, and loves you.

I — INFORM OTHERS

After you have become educated about being ADD and possibly received an official diagnosis, you may want to inform concerned others about what you have discovered. You will find

165

most people will have an "aha" moment just like you may have experienced. Others, however, may not be so accepting of even a valid explanation to your "quirkiness." Some of the people you may want to consider sharing your discovery with includes your spouse, children, parents, close friends, employer/employees, and pastor.

O — OPPOSE

There is little doubt that you have adopted the negative labels and words that people have spoken to you and about you all of your life. Remember, you may not have been the one to put the faulty pair of glasses on, but you are the one who is taking ACTION to remove them.

A critical part in removing the glasses is correcting and controlling your internal dialogue, or your self-talk. The ADDer becomes a pro at lying to himself. You must *oppose* negative statements and wrong labels placed upon you. This is much more than "positive thinking." This means considering how God sees you and how He made you. Anything opposed to the labels He has placed on you (which, according to His Word, are anything but negative as we are submitted to His will) is false, and needs to be replaced with truth.

166

N — NEVER GIVE IN, NEVER GIVE UP

Dealing with ADD is a lifelong process. God is not going to "heal" you of being ADD any more than He might heal the outgoing, vivacious, driven personality in your next-door neighbor.

Yes, He can heal the pain of the past, restore relationships, and give you wisdom in how to best live in a not-so-friendly ADD world. At times, however, you will doubt yourself and question whether being ADD is even real. You will wonder if all your efforts will really pay off. It is important to make your mind up to never give in to those negative thoughts, and never give up on who God created you to be. His purposes and calling on your life still exist—regardless of your past track record.

It is very likely that hurt, disappointments, poor decisions, and the like may have created a rough history, to say the least. The question is what you will do with the knowledge that you are receiving right now. God does not judge our pasts on the knowledge we gain today and neither should you. Even God cannot change your past. Rest assured, our God is concerned with the principle of faith over decisions of the flesh. You can choose today to be miserable or to become strong. The choice is yours as to which direction you will go.

You can choose today to be miserable or to become strong. The choice is yours as to which direction you will go.

167

I am reminded of the story of an old Cherokee who was teaching his grandchildren about life. He said to them, "A battle is raging inside me —it is a terrible fight between two wolves. One wolf represents fear, anger, envy, sorrow, regret, greed, arrogance, self-pity, guilt, resentment, inferiority, lies, false pride, superiority, and ego. The other stands for joy, peace, love, hope, sharing, serenity, humility, kindness, benevolence, friendship, empathy, generosity, truth, compassion, and faith."

The old man intently stared at the children. "This same fight is going on inside you, and inside every other person, too."

They thought about it for a minute and then one child asked his grandfather, "Which wolf will win?"

The old Cherokee replied, "The one you feed."

I choose to accept how God wired me. I am not defective. I am not broken. And because God lives in me, I do not have a deficit.

I look forward to riding into New Jerusalem, under my Creator's control, with Him holding the reins and directing my path. I want to live with Him throughout eternity alongside other wild men and women who were Affectionately Designed Differently.

You are one of these people! You were wired differently for a different purpose. You are understood, accepted, and not alone! Welcome! There are many, many others just like you who were created to live life in full color—proving that it is a small world after all.

APPENDIX A

144 Questions That Could Change Your Life

The following questions can help determine whether an individual might be ADD. The more questions answered in the affirmative, the higher the likelihood that the intended person may be ADD. Everybody will answer "yes" to some of the questions; however, the ADD Adult will consistently relate to the majority of the questions. For a more accurate evaluation, the spouse, parent, or other close individual should answer the questionnaire on how it relates to *the potential ADDer*.

Personal

- Do you have difficulty maintaining focus on tasks or conversations?
- Are you a daydreamer, often drifting off into "space"?
- Do you struggle with your self-image?
- Do you have nervous energy?
- Are you impulsive?
- Do you incessantly shake one or both legs, tap your fingers, fidget, or feel the need to pace or get up and leave during meetings or events such as church?
- Are you overly impatient with tedious tasks?

- Do you begin many projects but often fail to complete them?

- Do you at times become so hyper-focused on projects, video games, television, or the computer that you tune out everything and everyone?

- Do you have a problem with procrastination?

- Do you sometimes walk into a room and forget why you're there?

- Do you regularly lose your keys, wallet, or checkbook?

- Do you often lock your keys in the car?

- Do you leave cabinet doors open?

- Is every day a "new" day for you (you're quick to forgive and wipe the slate clean)?

- Are you drawn to addictive behaviors, including any of the following: drugs, alcohol, sex, pornography, gambling, excessive work, excessive caffeine, compulsive eating, compulsive shopping?

- If you have ever used stimulants, did you find that they helped you to calm down and focus, rather than made you high or on-edge?

- Are you a better driver when the car radio is on?

- Are you a worse driver when trying to carry on a conversation?

- Do you surf the radio stations in your car?

- Do you surf television stations?

- Does waiting in line irritate you?

- Are you a visionary, seeing farther down the road than most people?

- Are you unable to make or follow a list?

170

- Do you often live by the philosophy "It's easier to ask forgiveness than to ask permission"?

- Is it a struggle for you to maintain structure or routine in your life?

- Do you have poor hand-eye coordination?

- Do you find it almost impossible to do administrative work, or pay attention to details?

- Do you crash after big projects or events?

- Is your IQ above average?

- Are you more creative or imaginative than most people?

- Do you manage short projects better than long, drawn-out ones?

- Do you become bored easily?

- Do you feel that you have failed to live up to your full potential?

- Do you tend to make decisions and act on them impulsively?

- Do you solve practical problems quickly?

- Does driving soothe you?

- Do you love cars?

- Do you get the gist of things very quickly?

- Do you have difficulty organizing household-related tasks?

- Do you have difficulty delaying gratification?

- Do you often fail to consider the consequences of your actions?

- Do you feel hopeless regarding the future?

- Do you miss familiar exits when returning home from work or other routine places?

- Is your attention span adequate only when something is very interesting to you?

- Do you have trouble listening to or reading directions and instructions?

- Do you often speak without thinking?

- Do you often act without thinking?

- Is your living area messy?

- Are you easily overwhelmed by paperwork or other mundane requirements, such as paying bills, getting your car inspected, or making a doctor appointment?

- Do you depend on others to organize you in order to successfully complete something?

- Does your mind race at night making it difficult for you to fall asleep?

- Do you experience periods of low energy, especially early in the morning and afternoon?

- Are you often reluctant to engage in tasks that require sustained mental effort?

- Are you usually able to figure out where an author, speaker, or preacher is going in the first 20 minutes of a presentation or in the first few chapters of a book?

- Do you get easily frustrated and impatient when things are going too slowly?

- Do you require stimulation from things such as action movies and video games, buying items, being among lively friends, driving fast, gambling, or engaging in extreme sports or risky behaviors?

- Do you often blurt out answers before questions have been completed?

- Do you often interrupt people?

- Do you sometimes fail to read body language of other people?
- Is it difficult for you to maintain eye contact when engaged in a dialogue, staring off in another direction?
- As a child, were you often labeled as being dumb, lazy, or irresponsible?
- As a child, were you considered uncoordinated in sports?
- As a child, were you often accused of not working up to your full potential?
- Were you hyperactive as a child?
- Did you often feel lonely as a child?
- Do you have a family history of ADD or hyperactivity?
- Do you have a family history of substance abuse?

173

Educational

- Are you left-handed or ambidextrous?
- Do you have any learning disabilities such as dyslexia?
- When reading, do you find that you often have to reread a paragraph or an entire page because your mind wanders?
- Do you often start books but rarely finish them?
- When writing, do you frequently transpose letters or numbers?
- Do you have difficulty getting your thoughts on paper?
- Do you have sloppy handwriting?
- Are you a poor speller?
- Does your performance become worse under pressure when taking written tests?
- Are you smarter than you've been able to demonstrate?

- Were you considered an underachiever in school?
- Did you enjoy school as a child and teenager?
- Did you have frequent behavior problems in school?

Relational

- Does your spouse, or those closest to you, seem to stay frustrated or angry with you?
- Do you seek out pornography on the Internet?
- Are you drawn toward inappropriate relationships with the opposite sex?
- Does your spouse resent you for promises made but not kept?
- Do you have difficulty sustaining intimate relationships?
- Would you describe yourself as needing an unusual amount of sex?
- Have you been divorced more than once?
- Do you often get distracted during sex, even though you enjoy it?
- Do you have a child diagnosed as ADD or ADHD?
- Do you have difficulty sustaining long-distance friendships?
- Do you often fail to see the needs or activities of others as important?
- Are you unnecessarily curt or verbally abusive to others?

Financial

- Do you fail to balance your checkbook, preferring to check the balance online?

174

- Are you incapable of sticking to a budget?
- Do you pay unnecessary late fees, reconnect fees, or overdrawn fees?
- Do you often buy on impulse?
- Do you have difficulty keeping money in a savings account?
- Is your solution to financial problems to make more money?
- Do you often max out your credit cards?
- Do you have a poor credit rating?
- Are you good at making money, but poor at managing it?

Vocational   175

- Is your work area messy, consisting of "organized" piles?
- Are you much more effective when you are your own boss?
- Do you have difficulty sitting at a desk for long periods?
- Have you experienced frequent job changes?
- Do you have a poor work record?
- Do you often have trouble with rules, policies, or laws?
- Do you have difficulty organizing work-related tasks?
- Do you have to work double-time to make up for your inefficiencies on the job?
- Do you forget appointments?
- Do you often make careless mistakes at work?
- Are memos virtually impossible for you to read or write?

* Do you have trouble going through established channels or following proper procedure?

* Do you stay at odds with people at work?

* Do you have a record of insubordination issues?

* Do you enjoy certain aspects of your job that do not include paperwork?

* Do you have a chronic sense of underachievement in your career?

Social

* In social settings, do you find yourself anxious to leave?

* Are you particularly intuitive regarding other people and their intentions?

* Are you often considered cocky, obnoxious, rude, or insensitive in social settings?

* Are you either the life of the party or the party pooper?

* Do you lack social graces or manners?

* Do you feel like exploding inside when someone has trouble getting to the point?

* Do you have trouble assessing the impact you have on others?

* Do you often drop food on your clothes while eating?

* Do you have difficulty maintaining friendships?

* Do you often say whatever comes to mind without considering its impact?

* Do you often embarrass others?

* Do you remember faces, but not names?

Spiritual

* Do you prefer to listen to an audio presentation as opposed to reading the Bible?

* Is it easier for you to pray while walking, driving, or pacing as opposed to sitting still?

* Are you unable to maintain a regular devotional time with the Lord?

* Are you viewed as rebellious toward spiritual leaders?

* Are you often seen as less spiritual than others?

* Do you feel misunderstood or not accepted by church members, church leaders, or pastors?

* Are you often accused of being in rebellion toward God?

* Do you often feel that God is disappointed in you?

Conclusional

* Do people have a difficult time understanding you?

* Do you have a hard time understanding yourself?

* Do you feel as though something has to change or else?

* Are you ready for some answers?

* Are you ready to finally be understood?

* *Are you ready to live up to your full potential?*

If you answered "yes" to the majority of these questions, you are probably wondering how someone else "read your mail" so well. Rest assured, you are not alone. There are millions of other ADD adults out there. There are answers to your questions and solutions to your problems. Life doesn't have to be miserable. You can live up to your full potential starting *now* by understanding that you are not sick, broken, or stupid!

144 Success Skills That Could Change Your Life

The following is a set of suggestions that may be helpful in dealing with the challenges that can accompany being ADD. Although not all will apply to the need of each ADD individual, we hope you find them informative and beneficial. Remember, the key is to find what works and then do it!

179

Personal

+ Redefine yourself by your strengths.

+ Lead with those strengths.

+ Involve others (especially your family and close friends) in your ADD success strategies.

+ Make an effort to think before you speak or act.

+ Count to ten before you say something that might be taken wrong.

+ Plan in advance to direct your excess energy into positive channels.

+ Place your wallet, keys, and other personal belongings in the same place every day.

+ Get a GPS (Global Positioning System) navigation system to help with driving directions.

* Keep an extra set of keys at your home, office, and in your car.

* Install key code locks on your home, office, and car doors.

* Sign up with a travel service that will come and unlock your car should your keys get locked inside.

* Use the cruise control when driving through school zones or other speed traps.

* Use a PDA (Personal Digital Assistant) or computer for alarms to help with your to-do list.

* Have a non-ADDer enter car maintenance schedules, doctor appointments, anniversaries, birthdays, and other important events on your computer or PDA.

* Record your to-do list on your PDA, then print out a hard copy.

180

* Focus on what you are naturally good at and get help doing the other stuff.

* Exercise

* Allow yourself to take classes (sports, computer, art, etc.) that have a 3- to 6-month obligation versus ones that require a longer commitment.

* Hire a cleaning service.

* Hire a lawn service.

* Listen to books on CD rather than forcing yourself to read books.

* Get professional help if you feel an addictive draw toward any of the following: drugs, alcohol, sex, pornography, gambling, excessive work, excessive caffeine, compulsive eating, compulsive shopping, etc.

* Drive with the radio on, and warn those riding with you that you are a better driver with it on.

* Tackle jobs, chores, or projects in short increments.

* Don't allow others to lend you items such as books, CDs, or tools.

* Allow others to help create a semblance of routine in your life.

* Understand that after big events or projects that you will experience a "down" time and will need to crash.

* Schedule a crash day.

* Allow yourself to do what helps you to crash on crash days: going to the movies, playing video games, taking a nap, playing golf, running errands, etc.

* If you are having a "bad ADD day," don't hesitate to take the day off, crash, and hit it hard the next day.

* Set a timer to help with time management when watching television, playing video games, or using the computer for entertainment.

* Slow down when making big decisions.

* Don't make a big decision during an emotional time in your life.

* Readily own up to any poor behavior on your part.

* Use corkboards and white boards to help organize your life by posting bills, reminders, calendars, etc., on them. (If an ADDer can't see something such as a phone bill, then *it does not exist!*) Pull the bills and reminders down only after they've been completed.

* Train yourself to maintain eye contact with people.

* Make an effort not to interrupt people.

* Enlist others to give you signals when you are tempted to interrupt.

181

- Replace any negative labels placed on you by others (or by yourself) with positive and more accurate labels.

- Keep your self-talk in check. Make sure you are not lying to yourself in any way!

- Maintain healthy friendships.

- Find "white noise" that works for you such as a fan or music to help you stay focused.

- Give yourself permission to multi-task.

- If you know that you are unable to complete a job 100 percent, then figure out what percentage of the job you can finish and ask for help completing the rest.

- Find a counselor or a life coach to help deal with the more complicated issues surrounding ADD.

182

- Enlist an accountability partner, whether your spouse, a close and trusted friend, or pastor to help you with the daily challenges of ADD.

- Recognize that negative ADD characteristics can be exacerbated by stress.

- Give yourself credit for surviving thus far, despite being ADD.

- Limit the gadgets you use to stay organized: get one cell phone that is also a PDA—it can keep up with your contacts, appointments, to-do lists, and reminders. If your budget allows it, get one that includes a GPS system. The fewer items you have to keep up with, the better.

- Always get the insurance offered on things like cell phones in case you lose or break yours.

- Pay attention to your health—diet, exercise, checkups, etc.

- Be willing to try ADD medication if you find yourself paralyzed in *any* major area of life (job, school, relationship).

- Be willing to change medication or the dosage if it is not working for you, or if it is causing negative side effects.

- Be willing to try natural alternatives to medication; some can be very helpful.

- If you have difficulty sleeping at night, try non-stimulating activities such as reading or taking a hot bath versus watching television or playing video games.

- If you experience depression, anxiety, panic attacks, or anything else that can sometimes crop up alongside ADD, see your doctor immediately.

- Reward yourself for doing the right thing for the right reason.

- Learn to laugh at yourself.

- Allow others to express humor when ADD is obvious.

- Focus on finding solutions to your challenges rather than focusing on the problem.

Educational

- Sit toward the front of the class.

- Inform the instructor that you are ADD.

- Ask for books on CD rather than in written form.

- Ask the instructor for permission to either pace the back of the room or take short breaks.

- Ask the instructor about oral tests versus written tests.

- Partner with another student who can share notes.

- Record lectures.

- Do homework with some form of white noise running (e.g., a fan or even a radio).

183

- When reading a book, keep a pen handy to mark important parts and to jot down any thoughts that may come up.

- Place a bright orange poster board on the surface of your study area to help maintain your focus.

- Use a spell–checker, whether on the computer or by asking someone to read over your work.

- Don't beat yourself up for not finishing a book.

- Don't beat yourself up for reading several books at one time.

- If you can't type or you type poorly, buy a fun typing program for the computer.

- Don't sell yourself short when it comes to education. You are smart and can figure out a way to further your education. Again, look for solutions rather than focusing on the problems.

- Allow your accountability partner to help keep you motivated and on-track in your studies.

Relational

- Allow your spouse, your accountability partner, or those closest to you to offer reminders about important dates, events, tasks, and appointments.

- Give your spouse or close friend permission to hold you accountable in *all* areas.

- Negotiate chores and other tasks with your spouse or roommate.

- Be quick to apologize to your spouse, family members, or friends when blowing it.

- Make small, keepable promises to your spouse and family members.

- Be very willing to participate in holding Devotional Times (defined in this book) with your spouse.

- Give your spouse permission to remind you when a Devotional Time will be held.

- Be creative in where and how the Devotional Times are held (e.g., back porch, bathtub, while taking a walk, etc.) This will help you to maintain focus.

- Communicate clearly and openly with your spouse regarding your emotional needs.

- Identify and begin meeting the emotional needs of your spouse.

- Communicate clearly and openly with your spouse regarding your sexual needs and concerns.

- Discuss *any* new endeavors, ideas, and major changes with your spouse or accountability partner.

185

- Be upfront and honest with your spouse, family members, or close friends about your struggles with being ADD.

- If others in your family are ADD (your child or parent), offer them the same understanding and acceptance that others give to you.

- Don't allow ADD to become an excuse. Remember, it is an explanation, not an excuse.

- Don't allow yourself to become curt or verbally abusive to others.

- If inappropriate websites become an issue for you, allow your spouse, accountability partner, or close friend to put a filter on the computer where *they* retain the password.

- Listen to feedback from those who are invested in you.

- Verbally repeat dialogue back to the person you are speaking with to clarify points, requests, or instructions.

* Call your spouse when you are in the grocery store *and* before checking out to make sure you have everything you went there to get.

* Take mini-vacations with your spouse, even if only for one night in a nice hotel.

* If you are not yet married, look for a spouse who complements your uniqueness and is fully aware of your ADD.

* Be loyal and faithful to your spouse at *any* cost.

Financial

* Don't carry too much cash around.

* Minimize use of credit cards and check writing.

* Cut up credit cards that carry a high interest rate.

186

* Don't ask for or accept personal loans from friends or family.

* Don't ignore your financial situation; face your debt and stay aware of your credit report.

* Communicate with your spouse or accountability partner about large purchases.

* Give yourself 24–72 hours to think about a large purchase of any kind.

* Sign up for online banking so you always know where you stand in your account.

* Have your paycheck directly deposited into your bank account.

* Have your health and life insurance directly drafted from your account.

* Have a portion of your paycheck automatically deposited into your savings account.

* Allow your spouse, trusted friend, or a professional to help with your finances if you have problems in that area.

Vocational

* Explain your work habits to your coworkers (e.g., piles of stuff, easily distracted, think out loud, need white noise, etc.)

* Don't sit at a desk for long periods.

* Get a wireless phone and walk around while talking on the phone.

* Allow others to hold you accountable for keeping office policies and procedures.

* Use the gadget that works for you in keeping up with appointments, to-do lists, projects, and important events.

187

* If you are the boss, look for employees who balance your skills. If your weakness is spelling and organization, then look for the person who can help you in those areas.

* Be quick to apologize to your coworkers when you blow it.

* Don't feel locked into your current career. (However, if you decide to make major changes in this or any area, involve your spouse or accountability partner.)

Social

* Learn to relax and enjoy social situations.

* Look people in the eye.

* Make a point to observe other people's body language and facial expressions.

- Make a point to ask people questions about *their* families, interests, and so on.

- Allow your spouse or close friend to give you signals regarding social graces or manners.

- Learn to be patient with others as they are expressing their points of view.

- When dining, eat more slowly as to not drop food on yourself.

- When trying to remember names, associate something with the person's name and face that will help you remember them.

- Count to ten before you blurt something out.

- Remember that you do not always have to offer your opinion or have the last say.

Spiritual

- Understand that God wired you in a unique way for a unique purpose.

- Understand that if God created you this way, then it must fit into His plan for your life.

- Understand that although God may not always approve of your actions, He unconditionally accepts you.

- Understand that when God corrects you, He is not rejecting you.

- Find what draws you closer to God, and then do it (e.g., listening to the Bible on CD, praying while driving, spending time with the Lord while hiking).

- Use Bible computer programs to improve your study and devotional times.

- Do not beat yourself up for not having the same type of relationship with God that others have.

- Do not allow yourself to commit to long-term projects at church. Volunteer for shorter assignments that do not involve paperwork or follow-up.

- Ask God to bring other ADDers into your life so that you may help them.

- Encourage your church to begin an ADD-friendly Bible study.

- Help educate your pastor or other spiritual leaders about ADD by giving them a copy of *Welcome to Our World*.

Conclusional

- Remain educated on ADD: this will help when you (or others) begin to doubt if ADD is real or not.

- Help fellow ADDers to see the truth about how they were created by giving them the audio version of this book. Make it your *personal* ministry to help those who were created differently.

- Understand that we are *all* in process. Change takes time and no one gets it right 100 percent of the time.

- Let Phil and Cynthia Phillips know how this book has affected you and your life. Your words of encouragement will help them to help others. They can be contacted at www.ADDwelcometoourworld.com.

189

**Did you know research indicates that
less than 25% of children raised by Christian parents
will live for the Lord as adults?**

*The primary goal in Miracle Parenting is to help parents under-
stand and embrace their overall calling—the passing of their faith
to the next generation. In order for this generational transfer to
take place, Miracle Parenting helps parents practice the "process" of
blessing their children through unconditional acceptance, unconditional love, and meeting their children's emotional needs. Parents
also learn how to implement the four components in biblical discipline: training, teaching, correction, and reward.*

THE MIRACLE PARENTING GROUP STUDY COURSE contains the materials you need to offer this powerful training
course in your church, your home cell groups, or other practical
setting for large or small groups.

- **The high-quality 8.75" x 11.75", 288-page, hardbound
  *Leader's Guide*** contains the entire course content with study
  questions and devotional-time assignments presented in a
  user-friendly manner, making it easy to follow and share.

- **The high-quality 8.75" x 11.75", 144-page, hardbound
  *Participant's Manual*** corresponds with the Leader's Guide
  containing the core outline for every chapter, as well as devotional-time assignments. (Additional Participant's Manuals

may be obtained at a 70% discount through our website, www.miracleparenting.com, or by calling toll-free: 877-633-3005.)

- **The 4 included Leadership Training CDs** equip and prepare you to successfully conduct the Miracle Parenting programs as a group ministry.

- **The 16 teaching CDs** bring the course to life as Phil and Cynthia share personal illustrations along with in-depth biblical teachings to truly impact their listeners.

THE MIRACLE PARENTING INDIVIDUAL STUDY COURSE is the perfect solution for parents who wish to go through this powerful training course in the comfort and convenience of their own home, at their own pace.

- **The high-quality 8.75" x 11.75", 144-page, hardbound** *Individual Study Guide* contains the entire course content with study questions and devotional-time assignments.

- **The included 16 teaching CDs** bring the course to life as Phil and Cynthia share personal illustrations along with in-depth biblical teaching.

See how the lasting benefits of the Miracle Program
can change your family for generations to come!

Quick Order Form

Telephone orders: Call toll-free (877) 633-3005 to order. Have your credit card ready.
Fax orders: Fax this form to (972) 722-1721
Postal orders: Miracle Families, P.O. Box 2333, Rockwall, TX 75087
Order online: www.miraclefamilies.net

Title	Price	Quantity	Amount
ADD: Welcome to Our World Book	19.95		
ADD: Welcome to Our World Audio Book	24.95		
ADD: Welcome to Our World Book *(10 Pack)*	145.95		
ADD: Welcome to Our World Audio Book *(10 Pack)*	195.95		
Miracle Parenting Group Study Course	149.95		
Miracle Parenting Individual Study Course	99.95		

Shipping and Handling
(Add $5 for first item; $2 for each addt'l item. International orders, add $12 for first item; $7 for each addt'l item. *Free S/H for orders of $120 or more within the continental U.S.*)

TOTAL

☐ Please send more information about seminars on ADD.

☐ Please send more information about Miracle Parenting seminars.

☐ Please send information about personal life-coaching from Phil & Cynthia Phillips.

Name _____

Address _____

City _____ State _____ Zip _____

Country _____ Phone _____

E-mail _____

Method of Payment: ☐ Check/Money Order *(payable to Miracle Families)*
☐ Visa   ☐ MasterCard   ☐ AMX   ☐ Discover

Card Number _____ Expir. Date _____

Card Holder *(please print clearly)* _____

Signature _____